Kevin Desmond

The Man with Two Shadows

The Story of Alberto Ascari

PROTEUS

PROTEUS BOOKS is an imprint of
The Proteus Publishing Group

United States
PROTEUS PUBLISHING COMPANY, INC.
733 Third Avenue, New York
N.Y. 10017

distributed by:
THE SCRIBNER BOOK COMPANIES, INC.
597 Fifth Avenue, New York
N.Y. 10017

United Kingdom
PROTEUS (PUBLISHING) LIMITED
Bremar House,
Sale Place,
London, W2 1PT.

ISBN 0 906071 09 7

First published in US April 1981
First published in UK March 1981
(c) 1981 Kevin Desmond
All rights reserved.

Printed and bound in England
by The Pitman Press

DEDICATION

"To E.M., who suffered twice."

ACKNOWLEDGEMENTS

The Author wishes to thank the following for their help during the preparation of this book: Signora Mietta Ascari; Cesare di Agostini; Gilberto Colombo; "Corriere della Sera" (Archives Dept.); Luigi Fusi (Alfa-Romeo); R. N. Eason-Gibson; Denis Jenkinson; Louis Klemantaski; Ing. Aurelio Lampredi; Lancia (UK) Ltd; Count Gianni Lurani; Indianapolis Motor Speedway; Corado Milanta; Dr. Paolo Montagna; Stirling Moss; Pirelli; Cyril Posthumus; Gigi Villoresi; "Grande Vitesse".

Last but not least, my own two, long-suffering shadows - my wife Alex and my dog "Hengist".

FOREWORD

"Dear Alberto

Despite all that happened on that sad afternoon of May 26, I am incapable of saying goodbye to you. It seems you are still there, beside me. We spent so much of our lives together in the warm embrace of friendship, that everything seems to have stopped without you.

Do you remember the tests, the trials, the Grand Prix, the journeys, the chattering, the hours of rest? And the endless mutual decisions, because we felt that we shared the same journey in life?

You fell at Monza in sight of the race that for the first time would have seen us divided. I knew that this insignificant, even if brief, separation, displeased us both. It did not depend on us, it was circumstance, in the life of two racing drivers. Indeed this separation, right at the end of our career, left a shadow of regret...

That day, while we were at the bar of the Autodrome, and I saw you break off from our group, and arrive at Castellotti's car and put on a helmet, gloves, goggles and a vest that were not yours, I was astonished.

I knew, oh, so well from close at hand, your precision, the meticulous care in your preparation, which always had to be exemplary, like so many aspects of your make-up both as private man and public figure and yet you flaunted all your own rules. Evidently this was Destiny. You had been spared at Monte Carlo so that you could fall in some run of the mill drive.

This, Alberto, made separation all the more brutal. For this reason I still cannot find it in myself to say addios.
(Written and Published in 1956)."

"Re-reading "Caro Alberto" has disturbed me deeply however I would be more than happy for you to use this remembrance of mine of Alberto, as the Preface to your book on his life. The article was written by me, at that time, under the terrible weight of the tragic accident; I would be unable to say anything better today."

(From a letter sent to the Author in April 1980)

PRELUDE

On May 26 1955, a 25 year-old student from Milan, went up to
Monza with his Leica camera, with the intention of doing a
photo-study of the Royal Park and it's old buildings set in the
panorama of the Brianza countryside. It was a quiet, sunny day
perfect for photography. In the distance, the student could
hear the sound of a powerful car going round the motor-racing
circuit, which was a part of the Park. He listened to the high-
pitched yowl of the engine as the gears were swiftly and
efficiently changed...

Then the roar of the distant engine halted abruptly - there
was an ominous clank-clank-clank - then complete silence.
With a strange sense of foreboding, the student started to run -
only to come across an upturned, unpainted, un-numbered
racing car and nearby, its driver, lying in a pool of blood. He
saw people, deathly pale, running from the other direction. On
impulse, he framed the horror in the viewfinder, then took a
photograph then another, then another...

"That evening," he was to recall to me many years later, "I
sold those photographs and the negatives to an Italian
magazine and to 'Paris Match'. They paid me extremely well. I
am not proud of what I did, but in those days I was a student,
and I needed the money. I have never been interested in motor-
racing, but in the days that followed, I was to learn a great deal
about that crash, about the dying man I had photographed,
and about a particularly macaber chain of coincidences which
had linked his death to that of his father's....."

The driver's name was Alberto Ascari. His father's name was Antonio Ascari, named after St. Antonio of Padua, who died on June 13 1232. Alberto Ascari was *born* on June 13, and regularly lit a candle to that Saint. St. Antonio of Padua, Antonio Ascari and Alberto Ascari - were all 36 years old when they died. Antonio Ascari lived for 13,463 days and Alberto Ascari lived for 13,466 days - precisely three days longer than his father. Both men were killed on the 26th of the month (twice 13), both driving racing cars, both cornering to the left.

Could it be that this matrix of coincidences was a mere haphazard sequence? Or one of Destiny? Or were there deeper, more clandestine matters involved? Just who or what were those two shadows? To find the answers, we must search through the life histories of Antonio, then of Alberto Ascari, two of the World's greatest motor-racing drivers. Our story begins almost one hundred years ago......

CONTENTS

"The First Shadow"

Antonio Ascari was born on September 15, 1888 at "Moratica", four houses in the neighborhood of the tiny, clustered village of Bonferraro di Sorga, near the border dividing the Provinces of Verona and Mantua. Moratica was also quite near to the town of Casteldario, where some four years later, on November 16 1892, another great Italian racing driver, Tazio Nuvolari would be born. A border line is merely cartographic, and anyone in this region such as Antonio, the son of a grain and corn merchant - or Tazio, the son of a land owner, - would have come to speak in the Venetian dialect, tinged with Mantuan.

Antonio was just one among nine brothers and sisters, but from the start he showed himself of an independent frame of mind: Following an attempt to set light to the beard of his sleeping schoolteacher, the young Ascari's academic education came to an abrupt end, turning instead to a blacksmith's forge at Stradella on the Mantua-Casteldario road, where he learned to weld bicycle tubes. Here he joined the locals in enthusiastic admiration of the crack cycling champions - the Nuvolari brothers, Arturo and Guiseppe - and also reacted in wonderment to the arrival of a new form of transport - the motor car.

From Stradella, Antonio progressed to Casteldario and a job in the countryside where he learned how to service agricultural machinery only recently introduced. The teenage Ascari and the teenage Nuvolari may even have bumped into one another in the streets of Casteldario - as they would later do on the race circuits over a decade later.

Leaving behind the ease and intimacy of a small community, the Ascari family left the countryside and went to face the pace and noise of Milan, the city which, together with Turin and Genoa, was then leading a belated but dynamic Italian industrial revolution. By diligence and application, Antonio had soon been promoted from mechanic to the manager of the

Milan repairs depot of an Italian make of car long since forgotten - De Vecchi.

In 1909, Major Donato Morelli of Casteldario persuaded the 22 year-old Antonio to "Go West Young Man" across the ocean to Parà, Brazil and start up a concessionaire's office, an agency for De Vecchi. This he did with his favorite brother, Amedeo. But their South-American adventure proved a tragic mistake. Amedeo died of yellow fever in his brother's arms. Upset and dispirited, Antonio sold everything and returned home to the De Vecchi parent company in Milan .

In April 1911 he began motor racing by specially preparing a works De Vecchi and then driving it, with his friend Ugo Sivocci, in the Modena Six Days' Reliability Trial. After showing some considerable skill, he was forced to retire towards the end of the contest, a muted debut.

Just before the First World War, Antonio left De Vecchi, whose fortunes were dwindling. At the beginning of hostilities, he was repairing airplanes for the Government, in a company called Falco. But by the Armistice, Falco had returned to coachbuilding and Antonio had left them to set up a car agency for the Società Anonima Lombarda Fabbrica Automobili - or ALFA, for short, just before that company was taken over by sig. Nicola Romeo and became Alfa-Romeo. This agency of Ascari's, in Via Castelvetro, was to become one of the biggest in Italy and abroad, alongside such names as Concina of Rome and Presenti of Florence. It assured Antonio of an income which allowed him to go motor racing as a sportsman.

On June 13 1918, Antonio's wife Elisa, born on September 13 1888, precisely two days before her husband, gave birth to a baby boy called Alberto. The fact that Alberto had been born on the same day as St. Antonio of Padua, was considered by Antonio Ascari as something of a well-timed coincidence.

In 1919, Antonio attended a race, which Guiseppe Campari won, on the Cremona Circuit. Ascari accosted the winner immediately after the race, congratulated him and in effect challenged him by saying 'I can drive like that' - 'Maybe' was Campari's answer.

Antonio bought a 1914, 4.5. liter two-seater Fiat which had been built for the American circuit at Indianapolis, but never raced there. On October 5 1919, in fog and rain, Antonio won the classic Parma to Poggia di Berceto hillclimb - beating nine other competitors, including a 21 year-old called Enzo Ferrari driving a CMN. Most extraordinarily, he won it, cornering by braking, not by changing gear!

After the race, in a black raincoat, spattered with mud, he sat at the place of honor at the Poggia Hotel dining-room, enjoying a large plate of tagliatelle and the smiles of his admirers. Further down the table sat the disgruntled Alfa team, among them Guiseppe Campari, badly defeated in this race and muttering something about 'I'll challenge him soon, but don't hurry me.'

Antonio heard this, and at the end of the meal, he turned round to Memini, his racing companion and friend and said loudly "Before challenging me, he must demonstrate that he knows how to do that route in the time that I took!"

And, as if to rub it in, that same month this wealthy 31 year-old car dealer and passionate motorist, also won the Coppa della Consuma hill climb.

The 1920's were only just beginning and it looked as if Antonio could become on of Italy's promising new drivers.

On November 23, he competed for the Targa Florio, that notoriously wild and woolly race amidst the Sicilian mountains. Admittedly his South American experiences had prepared him for the surprises of rough, unmade roads, but the Sicilian conditions also presented him with snow, slush and mud.

After a good start, he reached Caltavuturo, 20 miles from the start, in 37 minutes. After some 32 miles, he had even overtaken some six cars. Then a little after Polizzi village the Fiat skidded violently in the snow and dived straight down a ravine, flinging out both Ascari and his companion Memini. It was said that he lay unconscious for over half an hour before searchers found him. His injuries, including a fracture of the right hipbone, were severe, and kept him out of racing for some months.

It was however, a most likeable trait of Antonio Ascari that no matter what the set-back, he would never back down; this straightaway endeared him to the Italian people. On June 13

1920, he was back, this time racing an Alfa Romeo on the Mugello Circuit - when the rear right wheel knocked against the post marking the 16th kilometer, at a cross-roads, the car going off course and overturning.

If 1920 had been an unsuccessful year, then 1921 was almost a waste of time, with Antonio beset by mechanical breakdowns in almost every race he competed in. In the Targa Florio he suffered the acute embarrassment of not even being able to compete because of chronic mechanical breakdown, just as he was about to approach the Starting Line! 1921 was a year when Enzo Ferrari, ten year's Antonio's junior was more successful than Antonio. Nevertheless, it was in that year that Antonio persuaded his Company to build the 20/30 ES sports-car which he called "my little lorry", as it gave him security.

Although 1922 hit him with further forced retirements, he was somewhat more successful in the Targa Florio contest, entering the fourth and last lap, just eleven minutes from the leader, the renowned Jules Goux. Ascari was forced to make his final tyre change only a mile or two from the finish. Whilst doing so, the jack, set up hurriedly and inaccurately, collapsed, and the car leaned over on its side. Helped by his faithful mechanic, Giulio Ramponi, an exhausted but determined Antonio succeeded somehow in physically lifting up the car with his arms so that the tyre change could be completed. But many precious minutes had been lost. Although they finished 1st in their Class, they were placed 4th overall.

One further event that year was to prove highly significant for Ascari. This was the construction of the 6.2. mile Monza Autodrome some 15 miles North of Milan, a track that combined high speed banking with an effective road circuit.

Watched by some 150,000 enthusiastic spectators, Antonio must have been bitterly disappointed at having to retire his 6 cylinder "RL" Alfa-Romeo just two laps from the finish of that very first Monza race. But from now on he would have a track, just fifteen minutes drive from either his home or business where he could practice and enjoy high-speed driving to his heart's content - and where, perhaps, he would soon be able to score a victory in front of a crowd of home supporters.

Yet in the eyes of his friends and of the Northern Italian public, the fact that Antonio Ascari was not yet as victorious as he wanted to be, did not seem to matter. He was known to be an energetic, enthusiastic gentleman-sportsman, a good business-man, simple, frank, open-minded - and above all a good friend, generous in the extreme. Behind the wheel he was a "garibaldino"; driving with panache and great daring, always pushing engine and tyres to their limit. It was felt that it would only be a matter of time before he was victorious as well. 1923 was the year of the RL Alfa-Romeo and began with an even harsher disappointment and acute frustration for Antonio and his mechanic, Guilio Ramponi, in that elusive Targa Florio contest.

On the fourth and final lap and after a frantic wheel change, only nine of seventeen starters remain. Great News! Number 10, Ascari is leading the race, with Sivocci hot in pursuit. Ascari appears from the green hills of Cerda, on the last-but-one bend on a road that must spell out victory. Then, without warning his Alfa engine dies on him - only 100 meters from the finishing post - a complete and utter, silent standstill. Can this be? Frenetically, Ramponi struggles to disconnect the offending magneto, whilst from the not too distant pits, Alfa mechanics and assistants run helplessly towards the car. The spare magneto fitted, the engine roars back into life and Ramponi, settled on the bonnet, holds it secure in his hands while Antonio and additional passengers, cross the line.

But now certain officials have regarded this arrival as "irregular" and ask Ascari to do it again. Furious at the prospect of being thwarted once again, he takes a curious spectator by the shoulders, spins him round, pushes him into the Alfa instead of Ramponi and roars off back to the Cerda corner. Just as he is doing so, he meets Sivocci coming the other way, on the road to victory......

Three weeks later, Antonio scored his first outright victory in the 3-liter "RL" Alfa-Romeo around the very fast circuit of Cremona, 45 miles south East of Milan, at an average speed of 83.3 m.p.h., with a top speed of 85 m.p.h. His racing number? Unlucky thirteen.

To prove to himself that he had broken his run of bad luck,

Antonio now followed up with a Class win in the gruelling Targa Mugello race near Florence on June 10 - again not without incident. Approaching a double bend, he was suddenly blinded by a cloud of dust. The Alfa "RL" left the road and ended up, precariously balanced, with its rear wheels teetering over a ravine; the mechanic, thrown out, was miraculously unhurt. But it took them fifteen minutes to get the car back on the road again. Thus Ascari was beaten by two counts, Brilli-Peri and Masetti, to 1st overall.

Now Nicola Romeo's great ambition had always been to build a Grand Prix racing car that would dislodge Fiat's stranglehold on Italian - and even European - motor racing. To this end, he recruited a team comprising engineer Giorgio Rimini - and drivers Ascari, Campari, Enzo Ferrari and Ugo Sivocci.

During early 1923, a 2 liter, 6-cylinder car, designated the P1, was created. But it was so powerful that during practice for the European Grand Prix at Monza early that September, Ugo Sivocci was fatally injured when his P1 crashed. Immediately the remaining P1's were withdrawn from the Grand Prix entry, and for Alfa-Romeo it was back to the drawing board.

Almost immediately afterwards, on his own initiative, Enzo Ferrari paid a visit to Turin and suggested to a member of Fiat's design team, a certain Vittorio Jano, 33 years-old, of military extraction, that he might like to head the design team at Alfa Romeo that could produce the P2. After further words with Giorgio Rimini, Jano agreed to leave Turin for Milan and start work.

By setting up an almost military regime at Milan, as early as October 10 1923, Vittorio Jano had completed much of the P2 engine design and drawings. The P2 was to be something altogether new, a departure for the Milan company, because for the first time, they were attempting an 8-cylinder super-charged machine - a fantastic power potential. If things went according to plan, the P2 prototype would be ready for testing around Monza by early Spring.

But first, for Antonio Ascari, there was a jinx to overcome in the shape of the 1924 Targa Florio contest. 37 entries, and he who is leader after five laps also wins the Coppa Florio - shield and cup presented by Vincenzo Florio himself. April 27, race day, was a Mediterranean scorcher and saw Werner on a Mercedes going into the lead, with Ascari on a 3.6 liter Alfa, hot in pursuit and catching up fast.

On Ascari's appearance on the final bend, the mass of spectators go wild with cheering in the knowledge that here is their Italian, only 27 seconds behind Werner and with 50 meters to go - secure that Italy will defeat Germany.

Then, unbelievably, it happens again. Some 50 meters from the finishing post of a 268-mile race which has taken over six and a half gruelling hours to complete, the Alfa spins round in the dust and sputters to a halt. In desperation, Ramponi throws himself on the starting handle - but in vain, because the gear lever has been twisted. Ascari even tries to start the car by putting it into reverse gear, with success, but only putting himself further away from that Finishing Post.

In the meantime, organizers, officials and spectators run towards the inanimate car. Ascari climbs out and attempts to push a car weighing several hundred pounds *uphill*. With Werner roaring past triumphantly on the Mercedes, the Alfa is manhandled over the line with the help of numerous spectators and even soldiers. It is timed as finishing 2nd, but is subsequently disqualified for receiving "outside" help, so that Masetti is placed 2nd, Bordino 3rd and Campari 4th.

Sitting on a box, in the corner of his pit, a bitterly frustrated Ascari, turns to Ramponi, and with tears in his eyes, exclaims, "Guilio, Guilio! Go and find another driver, because if you stay with me you'll never have the satisfaction of winning a race! All I've done is make a reputation as the idiot that won't give up!"

Antonio's only consolation was a telegram from Nicola Romeo. It read: "This day of passion will remain engraved on my heart. The amazing tenacity and determination shown today has placed you and your colleagues even more firmly within my affections. Thank you dear friends, for adding new laurels to the victory wreath. Romeo."

The first P2 car, Vittorio Jano's masterpiece, was completed by the end of May. Ascari and Campari were appointed its test-drivers in a series of unpublicized running-up trials carried out round the Monza circuit, followed by runs over the Parma-Poggio di Berceto road - where on May 11th, Antonio had recently scored a victory driving the "RL" Alfa-Romeo, doing one lap at 84 m.p.h., and beating Materassi in an aero-engined Itala by just four and a half seconds.

Then came the race on the 200-mile Circuit of Cremona, with its long 6-mile straights. The P2 made its first official public appearance - its bare metal bodywork, unpainted and unvarnished - with Ascari at the wheel and Luigi Bazzi, of the P2 design team, as his riding mechanic. Arriving only the evening before, Ascari not only won the race, lapping at 98.3m.p.h., but was clocked through the 6-mile straight at 121.16 m.p.h., a phenomenal road speed for 1924! For two hours, Antonio Ascari showed an astonished and delighted public that this was the car to be reckoned with.

One month later, Ascari went to France for his first Grand Prix race abroad, on the 14-mile Lyons circuit. His team-mates were Campari and Wagner - a P2 trio. The sinuous Lyons circuit, a road triangle comprizing Givors, Mornant and Sept Chemins presented drivers with a winding valley road, a straight main road, a mountainous and rough secondary road, a switchback and steep descent to a nasty hairpin. Ascari, Campari and Wagner, in their P2 Alfas were up against the best of Europe's GP cars and drivers: Sunbeams driven by Segrave, Guinness and Resta; Delages driven by Divo, Benoist and Thomas; Bugattis, and a Fiat 805 driven by the great Bordino.

After a rolling start behind a motor-cyclist under a clear summer sky, Segrave's English Sunbeam shot into the lead, with Ascari close behind. Then Segrave lost the lead to Bordino, who now had to do battle with Ascari - Fiat versus Alfa Romeo. But then Bordino had serious brake trouble - and Antonio took his chance and went into the lead, lapping at over 75 m.p.h.

On Lap 16, he took 4 minutes for a refuel and a re-tyre, thus letting Guinness's Sunbeam into the lead, closely pursued by Campari in the other P2, just 20 seconds behind. Then Guinness stopped to change a wheel and Campari went into the lead - but not for long. By Lap 20, Antonio had again overtaken his teammate.

Number 3 leads Number 10, but they are both P2s, both Alfa Romeos, both Italian red. Romeo, Rimini, Bazzi, Jano and the rest of the Alfa team relish this glorious feeling for another twelve laps, being at leisure to tell their drivers, via pit signs, that they may even slow down a little, as their nearest threat, Divo on the Delage, is almost three minutes behind them.

But then Fate was again cruel to Antonio Ascari. With only three laps to go, the P2 slows down and he is forced into the pits. They fill up with water. But then the car will not re-start. Not again! Together with the faithful Giulio Ramponi, Antonio tries desperately to re-start that engine, by pushing the car, by swinging the start-handle - by pushing and swinging, until sheer exhaustion forces them to give up, and they flop down, wracked in limbs and lungs, beside their silent car -water trickling feebly from its exhaust pipe, showing that the offending object was a cracked cyclinder block. Only too aware of his public failure, Antonio suddenly bursts into an uncontrollable fit of tears, whilst Giuseppe Campari and his mechanic, Attilio Marinoni, pass into the lead in their P2 to win the race at 70.97 m.p.h. - after seven hours and 502 miles of driving.

Presented with flowers, and a ridiculously long 6-foot salami sausage - a gift from Lyons - the Alfa-Romeo drivers, including Antonio regarded as the "moral victor" made their triumphal entry back into Milan by train, and messages of congratulation were chalked on the side of their railway carriage.

Soon afterwards, Fiat announced their withdrawal from GP racing, having decided that the costs outweighed the benefits, and somewhat annoyed at having their ideas and designers "stolen" and better developed by other companies. From now on, with their P2 cars, Alfa-Romeo could become *the* Italian motor-racing company.

Antonio had to wait ten long weeks before he was able to redeem his reputation - his chance was to be on the home track, round Monza Autodrome in the Italian Grand Prix. They were weeks of concern at the Alfa-Romeo factory and of high-speed trials round the track; this time he could not afford to be let down. His only opponents in this contest were four supercharged Mercedes - one of them driven by a young man called

Alfred Neubauer, and another by the colorful Count Louis Zborowski, whose somber black racing costume contrasted strangely with the red silk shirts of the "Alfisti" drivers.

And it was the Count's strange death that gave Antonio Ascari the superemely popular victory he had so long desired. Strange, only if you know the facts...

In 1903, the Polish Count, Eliot Zborowski (whose idea it had been for each nation competing in Grand Prix races to be allocated a different color - red for Italy, blue for France, green for England, white for Germany) was competing in a white Mercedes at the La Turbie hillclimb contest, near Nice, when, tragically, as he came very fast into the first left-hand bend, his cuff-linked sleeve caught the hand-throttle of the Mercedes, flinging it wide open. The machine skidded uncontrollably into the rocks at the side of the road, and Zborowski was killed instantly.

Twenty years passed, before Eliot's son, Count Louis Zborowski started to make a name for himself, racing round Brooklands, England's banked concrete racing circuit in Surrey, in huge aero-engined cars which he called *Chitty-Bang-Bang*. Recalling his father's death, Lou would show his close friends the gold cuff-links that Count Eliot had been wearing at La Turbie, adding that for all the tea in China, he would never wear them himself, nor would he ever drive for the Mercedes team. That was tempting fate.

Then, sometime in 1924, Lou, suffering from an extremely disturbing emotional entanglement with a woman, signed up with Mercedes. Moreover, he turned up at the Monza Autodrome, the cuffs of his black shirt, held together by his father's ill-fated gold cuff-links.

On lap 8 of the Italian Grand Prix, Antonio Ascari's P2 Alfa overtook Lou Zborowski's Mercedes. 8 laps later he overtook Masetti's Mercedes. 8 laps after that, Zborowski was dead. Three 8's. His Mercedes had skidded on a patch of oil at the Lesmo Curve and rammed into a tree at high speed, killing Zborowski instantly. Following this, the entire Mercedes team was withdrawn, leaving the four P2 Alfa-Romeos to a high-speed walkover. Indeed their pace was so fast that towards the end of the race, Arturo Mercanti, who had conceived the

THE MAN WITH TWO SHADOWS

Autodrome and was its racing director, became terrified by the way in which Antonio Ascari was taking a particular corner so finely that he was throwing up the sand lining the edge of the track. So Mercanti sent a message to the Alfa-Romeo pit. It read: "If Ascari continues to take both large and small corners in a way dangerous to himself and others, I shall be constrained to stop him."

But, despite frantic pit signals to make him slow down, Antonio continued the pace, a broad, confident smile on his face. At the end of the race - throughout, a certain winner - he explained his tactics: "I was going fast on purpose, grazing those sandbags because it was the only position where the others were not going and there was no oil there."

But victor he was and nobody could dispute the fact. Five hours of high-speed driving at an average 98.7 m.p.h., with his fastest lap at a stunning 115 m.p.h., breaking World Records from 400-800 Km, some of them untouched for four years. Monza had become the fastest track in the World - faster even than the Indianapolis "Brickyard" circuit in the USA.

Antonio Ascari, the generous "Veronese di Milano" had become the motor-racing idol of Italy.

He still, however, had to score a victory, *away* from home, on foreign soil. In 1925, a World Championship series of races offered to give him that chance, incorporating races at Spa-Francorchamps in Belgium and then round a newly con-structed, banked circuit at Montlhéry, France. Consequently, he spent that Spring, checking-out and familiarizing himself with both venues.

Spa-Francorchamps, South-East of Liège and nestling in the Ardennes Mountains, was an open countryside, rough road, hairpin-infested course. It was to here, that in June 1925, Alfa-Romeo sent Ascari, Campari and their new team-mate, Gastone Brilli-Peri. Their only competition was a fleet of four, blue, supercharged Delages, driven by Divo, Benoist, Thomas and Torchy, tipped as "Queens of the track."

The race turned out to be a French farce, one of the dullest of races from the Belgian spectators' point of view. Because Antonio Ascari took the lead from the start and held it until the finish of the 900-mile, 54-lap, 6 and a half hour race, followed by the only other car to last the distance, his team-mate Campari - both men having plenty of time in hand for pit stops.

Given that from 1925, riding mechanics were no longer carried in Grand Prix races, it must have been a disappointment to Giulio Ramponi that he was unable to share the cockpit of that victorious P2 car.

As one by one, the Delages retired with mechanical trouble, the Belgian crowd, from a cold indifference, started whistling, booing and jeering at the successful Italians. This annoyed Vittorio Jano, who flagged in the three Alfa-Romeos and ordered their drivers to climb out and eat, ostentatiously, carefully timed five-minute snacks at a table in front of the pits, and in full view of the spectators, while the mechanics cleaned and polished the P2's until they shone - thus rubbing in the superiority of the Milan House of Portello.

On his arrival at the finish, a tricolor was draped over the bonnet of Antonio's car and a proud Giulio Ramponi prepared to give the victor his much photographed, checkered cardigan. The Alfa-Romeo team returned again in triumph to a crowded Milan station. Within the sea of admirers, was a 6 year old boy, jostled by the crowd, trying to make room for himself so that he could embrace and congratulate his father. The boy's name was Alberto Ascari.

During the weeks before his second challenge, at the Montlhéry circuit, Antonio was a man with ambitions. Among them was the possible realization of a long-term dream: that of constructing a car bearing his own name. Indeed, he had not only asked a friend of his, called Soresi, based in New York, to obtain an American Miller car, but was also planning to buy a building site in Milan where he would have his own factory. It should be remembered that, from the proceeds of his car agency, Antonio Ascari was not a man without considerable wealth. It must have appeared as an even stronger incentive to learn that, for the first time in European racing, whoever came in victor in the French Grand Prix at Montlhéry, would win 150,000 Francs - no small sum in those days, for someone considering starting up a car-manufacturing business.

But then, unexpectedly, things began to go wrong. On July 10, Gastone Brilli-Peri, whose experience and skill Antonio rated alongside his own, overturned his P2 in practice, escaping miraculously unharmed. Then Sozzi, Alfa's reserve driver, also had an accident, injuring his left arm. This unnerved Antonio Ascari.

Rather like Monza, the Autodrome of Linas-Montlhéry, some fifteen miles south of Paris, consisted of a high-speed banked track linked into a road cicuit. The 1925 French Grand Prix, to be held on the 7.7 mile road circuit, including the northern turn of the banked track, had been fixed by the Automobile Club of France (ACF) for July 26 1925.

With an unexplainable, heavy sense of foreboding, Antonio left his family at their country home, the Villa Solcio, beside Lake Maggiore, for the last time, on Friday, July 17; to those who are supersititious - an unlucky day of the week coupled with an unlucky number. On his arrival at Montlhéry, appointed Captain of the Alfa-Romeo team, he found himself unable to sleep for more than one or two hours every night. Maybe it was the noise of the French traffic and merrymaking in Linas. Maybe it was impatience to have done with a race round a circuit of which he disapproved.

One of the things which had disturbed him was a palisade, a wooden fence, about as high as a racing car, stretching right the way round the circuit - made up of wooden stakes, held together by wire. Stakes which would have been regular, if they had not been further supported by large, rough-hewn posts, hammered into the ground every two or three yards. Antonio himself had asked that these palisades be removed. They were a hazard to any driver cutting his corners as finely and as quickly as Antonio liked to.

"This circuit," remarked Antonio "presents difficulties and hazards that are useful to neither men nor machines. Along only two stretches and up on that splendid banked section can you do anything approaching 124 m.p.h. For the remainder of the track, you must slow down and be very careful you don't go off the track. But let's be patient, and we can't go wrong!"

During the practice the day before the race, Ascari appeared quieter than his usual self - almost morose. That evening, instead of going to bed early he went to the garage where Giulio Ramponi was working on the modified P2. Uncharacteristically

Antonio hovered around his mechanic, continually asking him questions, until Ramponi was provoked into saying, "Look, what's the matter? Don't you trust me or something?" To which Antonio, shocked by such a rebuke, went up to Ramponi, put his arm around his shoulder and muttered, "If you, Giulio, are also nervous tonight, then we're both in trouble." That night, Engineer Rimini found Ascari a quieter room where he could sleep better. He turned up the following morning, unshaven, wearing sandals and impatient to get out on the track. He explained that he couldn't be bothered to shave and that he was wearing sandals just in case he had to get out of his car in an emergency. Without waiting for either Campari or Brilli-Peri, Antonio drove off in the direction of the Autodrome like a man in a hurry.

The start at 8.00 a.m. on a cloudy, windy French morning, saw three Vl2 Delages, three 6-cylinder Sunbeams, five Bugattis and the three Alfa-Romeo P2's revving up on the starting line for the 620-mile race - the longest one-day event yet held in the motorsport world. When the flag fell, despite his nervousness, Antonio Ascari, Racing Number 8 roared away from the pack of cars and took a head-on lead, watched by almost 30,000 people, lining the circuit, who began to enjoy his style and to cheer him as he roared round, only a few feet from the top of the banking at a speed of at least 120 m.p.h., to disappear down the straightaway before anybody else had come into sight. With the energy and vigor so characteristic of him, Antonio now proceeded to build up his lead, distancing himself from his team-mate Campari by one minute, then by two, then four, then six minutes, then seven. It was his greatest drive.

At about 10 o'clock, on lap 15, he came into the pits for a pre-arranged fuel stop, which included changing the rear wheels. While waiting, he asked both Rimini and Jano how he was doing.

"You're first with seven minutes' lead and Campari is 2nd."

"So we're doing well!"

"Extremely well, so much so that you could even slow down the pace. You did one lap at 5 minutes 39 seconds. Don't force it any more. You can do it easily in six minutes. Slackcn off a little."

This advice annoyed Antonio, who was in the process not only of redeeming his honor, lost a year before at Lyons, but also of thoroughly underlining the supremacy of the P2. "Calm? I'm supposed to be calm? I am certainly calmer than you in the pits. Remember, I have often said that I'm not like Quintus Fabius Maximus, the Delayer. Win or lose this war, I refuse to hold back."

While saying this, he munched a Zabaglione (an egg-flip with Marsala Wine), threw two bananas into the cockpit, next to what he called his "Oriental Commodities" - thermos of champagne and water, and a fire extinguisher - resting on the racing mechanic's empty seat. Then he climbed back in himself and, having lost only two minutes, resumed his lead! On his reappearance, even the French public appeared to cheer and applaud him again.

On lap 20, it started to rain. On lap 21, he was timed at 5 minutes 58 seconds - and on lap 22, like a precise clock, he lapped at exactly 6 minutes. But now it was raining, and he should have slowed down more.

Then on lap 23, Antonio Ascari was very late. The Alfa Romeo pit staff frowned over their stopwatches, and looked up anxiously towards the banked section of the track. Then the loudspeaker at the Grandstands announced, "Car Number 3, the Alfa Romeo of Signor Campari, has overturned. The driver has been injured."

But then a strange thing happened. Car Number 3, Campari in the cockpit passed the pits and grandstand in perfect high-speed fashion, obviously in the lead. Relief - then a sudden, terrible realization, hastily confirmed by the loudspeaker that "the crashed car is in fact that of Number 8 - driven by Signor Ascari."

It was at the end of the 9th kilometer, at the slightly up-hill left-hand curve of the Hostelry of Saint Eutrope, that he came to grief. Speeding out of the straight that passed the water tower, Ascari entered that already slippery corner at between 110 and 120 m.p.h. As he did so, his nearside rear wheel knocked against - just grazed - one of the larger posts holding up that palisade fence - or to be more precise, his hubcap knocked against a protruding knot of a roughly hewn wooden post. The car skidded outwards and sideways - Ascari correcting too vigorously - so that the nearside rear wheel now proceeded to root up more than 60 yards of wooden fence, which gathered underneath the car, so locking the wheel, making the car go berserk, somersaulting twice, crushing Ascari and finishing up a bloody wreck, its wheels in the air, in the shallow ditch separating the spectators from the track, with Ascari pinned underneath it. The slow motion description of a matter of seconds.

Struggling like a rabbit in a metal trap, poor Antonio tried to free himself from underneath his car. His right leg was almost severed, the other leg broken, a broken arm, with severe and bloody head wounds.

His first rescuers were hopelessly slow in arriving. It is even reported that the official doctor took half an hour to arrive. Mechanics tried to bandage the leg to stop its profuse bleeding. From Antonio's lips there came a faint moaning. They laid him on a stretcher and took him to the Hostelry of Saint Eutrope, where the doctors, realizing the seriousness of the situation, ordered immediate amputation of the leg and transportation to the Piccini clinic in Paris.

Despite all his wounds, Antonio jerked violently as they put him into the ambulance, with only Memini and Ramponi at his side. At high speed, the ambulance started its journey towards Paris, but as they went through the town of Linas, Antonio shuddered violently - and died. The ambulance was turned round and at a slow pace, the body was taken back to Alfa-Romeo's Headquarters villa, where a mortuary room was made ready.

The race had continued with Campari in the lead, easily first. Then as Antonio's friend and closest rival, this huge man, made his second pit-stop to refuel, Vittorio Jano approached him and told him the bad news. Campari burst into tears. The emotion spread. Crying like children, the Alfa-Romeo team withdrew from a race that had been theirs for the taking - but not before they had run up their engines to show the public that nothing was wrong with them.

After the race, two drivers Benoist and Wagner, first and

second respectively, drove down to the spot where Ascari had crashed and laid their victors' garlands of flowers by the broken palisade.

In the mortuary room at Linas, for the rest of that sad day and the following morning, the French people filed past Antonio Ascari's body, resting as it was on white satin cushions and dressed in the red silk Alfa-Romeo racing shirt in which he had scored his great victories; the lower part of his body was covered with the tricolor flag.

Just before the oak coffin was closed, Arturo Mercanti, of the Automobile Club of Milan, kissed Ascari's forehead and said, "You will always be present amongst us." On the coffin lid was a little plaque. It read: "Antonio Ascari. Died at Linas (France) on 26 July 1925. For the Honor of Italy Abroad."

Among the rumors that were circulating, was one which claimed that a French "chauvinist" (Nationalist) had thrown a coil of barbed wire between the wheels of the Italian car, so that it would not win. The barbed wire was seen by everyone, between those wheels, but nobody could know with certainty whether it was the cause of the accident or not.

After a service at Linas Church, Antonio's coffin was taken to the Gare de Lyons, thence by train towards Italy, accompanied by his brothers Giuseppe and Vittorio Ascari and by his nephew, Minozzi. At every station it stopped at, this funeral train was loaded with more and more flowers.

At Bardonecchia, on the Italian border, highlander and lowlander alike, young and old, even children - further loaded that train with wild Alpine flowers. To Turin, then to Milan, where it arrived, its first two carriages crammed over-full with sweet-smelling blooms and with ribbons bearing the tricolors of both France and Italy. Among the more noticeable wreaths was one from Italy's new dictator. It read: "To The Intrepid Ascari, Mussolini". Followed by an immense crowd, the coffin was then taken to Portello House, the Alfa-Romeo building, to a mortuary room, adorned with a large silver cross, with silver-fringed black velvet curtains and with a large Italian flag. Through here, many of them sobbing, filed the people of Milan, to take a last look at their motor-racing idol.

The following day, the funeral cortege, an almost endless

row of black cars, crammed full of flowers, followed a prepublicized route through the city, in the direction of the Monumental Cemetery. The whole length was lined with thousands of mourners. In the car, nearest the hearse, Antonio Ascari's closer family: his widow, Eliza, her pale, tragic face, hidden by a long veil, accompanied by her brothers-in-law, Giuseppe and Vittorio - then there was Antonio's daughter, Amedea, and his son - Alberto - then the rest of the family. After them, followed all the personalities of Italian motorsport Romeo, Rimini, Jano, Campari, Brilli-Peri, Bordino, Nazzaro, Salamano, Ferrari - and a host of others. It seemed like the whole of Italy paying their last respects.

The Monumental Cemetery, that city of shrines and chapels, lying to the North-West of Milan, is an acreage of Lombardy where the wealthy "Milanese", city merchants and business-men, have been able to realize their desire to perpetuate their newfound wealth beyond Death. Each tomb is a sculptural edifice in itself, and each one evidence of an extreme attempt to differentiate one family from another.

It was at the back of this fantastic array of mausoleums, that Antonio Ascari, the wealthy car dealer, came to rest on the afternoon of July 30 1925. Standing by the grave, holding onto Giulio Ramponi's hand, was the 6 year-old Alberto Ascari, his big eyes looking out of a sad little, tear-stained face, trying to understand that he would never see his father again...

Soon after, the French put up a memorial to Antonio, a bronze bust, wearing goggles, at the very point on Montlhéry circuit where his last victorious race had been abruptly halted, re-naming the curve, Ascari Corner.

But it was not a family tomb in the Monumental Cemetery, or a memorial at Montlhéry, which would in future keep the name of Ascari alive. Instead it would be the exploits of that little boy - exploits that would not merely emulate the father, but would excel him to the very end.

"Antonio's Son"

1924: a blazing hot day, the temperature soaring into the 90's, the air of Monza Autodrome shuddering to the thunder of open exhausts. Alfa-Romeo are out, testing their P2 cars, the fastest in Antonio Ascari's capable control. Three times, his red car tears round the track and when he comes into the pits, Antonio nods his head to Vittorio Jano in satisfaction. Then he strips off his goggles and catches sight of his five year-old son, Alberto, eyes sparkling with excitement.

"All right then, in you get," Antonio orders with a smile, pointing at the driving seat. "That's all you've ever wanted to do since you crawled out of your cradle!"

Hardly daring to believe what he has just heard, the boy does as he is told, almost disappearing beneath the scuttle in the stark Alfa's cockpit, while his father shifts over into the mechanic's seat. "Off you go, son", the father says to his son, "Slowly now!" Watched by the highly amused group of Jano, Campari, Ramponi and others, Alberto Ascari drove off towards his first corner and his first lesson in motoring. That lap round Monza remained a vivid experience. It was the climax to a childhood spent 'pretending' he was a racing driver, holding an imaginary steering wheel and making 'engine noises' - the climax to a childhood spent alongside Monza track, amongst mechanics near the roar of engines, the pungent smell of burnt oil and the roar of a crowd that was cheering his father. These were memories which would continue beyond the unhappy void left by his father's death at Montlhéry, one year later.

His first education was at an Elementary School in Via Pietro Moscati, half a minute's walk from their family house in Corso Sempione. Here, taught by Fascist Captain de Filippo, he was one of the thousands of "Balilla", the Fascist Youth Movement, training in marching and gymnastics.

Then, one September day in 1929, when only eleven years old, Alberto saw in front of their house, a magnificent and new motorcycle. Watching its owners attempts to start it, with deafening explosions, the boy secretly promised himself that he would "borrow" it at the first available opportunity. Which is what he did - without, of course, obtaining permission first - and wobbling precariously, motorcycled down the streets of Milan and out into a large square usually used for military parades - fortunately to return without any mishap.

From then on, Alberto wanted to own his own motorcycle. Not far from their house, was a mechanic's shop which hired out motorcycles at a very reasonable price. Alberto also knew that for only 10 lire, he could get onto Monza Autodrome. So, using any pretext whatsoever - real or imaginary - the boy began to obtain money from his mother, Signora Eliza Marelli Ascari. He even played poker with his schoolmates to increase these savings. Each time he had saved enough, the young teenager hurried over to the mechanic's shop, hired out the fastest machine available and took the road to Monza. Once on the track, he did lap after lap until an empty petrol tank forced him to stop.

Before long, his mother had found out he was using his money and spare time on things she now disapproved of. Determined that her son would not take after her late husband in that respect, Signora Eliza, now something of an introspective, reserved woman, sent the 16 year-old boy off to a boarding school in Arezzo, Tuscany - some 200 miles from Monza. She had already sent her daughter, Amedea, off to a boarding school in Switzerland. At Arezzo, Alberto became homesick and bored, uninterested in his studies; one day, he plucked up enough courage to run away. Still wearing his boarding school uniform, he took the train north to Milan. But, despite tears and protestations, his mother sent him back to Arezzo. Soon after, fearing that her son might run away again, Signora Eliza sent him even further away, to the Scientific School in Macerata - this time 260 miles from Monza, where the discipline was twice as rigorous as in Arezzo. This only had the opposite of the desired effect. Again he ran away, back to Milan by train. On arrival, he went to a cafe and phoned his mother. "Mama, if you send me away again, I shall never return home. All I want to do is to race motorcycles."

Signora Eliza was obliged to give in and Alberto, in his 4th school year, was able to abandon his studies, with his final exams in sight. But from that date began his career as a professional racer. With the proceeds from the sale of his gold chronograph, his schoolboy savings - and also helped by a tangible contribution from a resigned mother, on the advice of two motorcyclist friends, Silvio Vailati and Nino Grieco, the 18 year-old Ascari bought his first motorcycle, the latest twin-cylinder 500 c.c. Sertrum.

With this, on June 28 1936, he made his first sporting appearance in the 24 hours of Alta Italia - a long test of regularity across Northern Italy. On his arrival on the first hairpin bend of Cisa Hill, Alberto took his first tumble, fortunately without damage. When he reached the suburbs of Pisa, his rear brake failed on him just as he was taking a corner. The motorcycle went berserk, jumped a ditch and Alberto ended up, unharmed, in a tomato field. The motorcycle was a write-off. Rather than deter him, this only fanned the flames of his desire to win, and the Sertrum was sent back to Milan by train.

From that moment, Signora Eliza understood that, after an interval of eleven years, her sad life of anxious waiting had been resumed.

Six days later, having repaired his machine, he scored his first victory, by winning in his class in a regularity test on the Lario Circuit; a victory which, because it was his first, would always remain sweet in his memory.

During the next five years that followed, Alberto Ascari (hair parted in the middle, piercing brown eyes, prominent teeth, white braces) was to learn a great deal. Two-wheeled racing - as such great drivers as Varzi and Nuvolari had learnt before him - requires great courage and a fine feeling for balance. On four wheels, one can usually correct mistakes to a certain degree without having an accident; on two wheels, it's harder.

1937 saw him become part of a racing "stable" - a "Scuderia Ambrosiana", where he was racing alongside such team-mates as Silvio Vailati and Nando Balzarotti, on 500 c.c. Class Gilera motorcycles, prepared by Mario Asso's G.R.F. in Milan.

Flaunting an ostentatious, great white leather coat with blue and black criss-cross bands on the front and back, "the son of the great Antonio Ascari" took part in twelve races, scoring five 1sts and two 2nds - with a particularly memorable performance in the 540 mile Milan-to-Taranto run that May, where on a standard sprung Gilera, he forced some of Italy's more notable riders to retire on their specially prepared machines, unable to keep up with his pace.

At the end of that season, he signed a contract with Bianchi and became one of their "works" riders, alongside Aldo Rebulgio and Guido Cerato - at 300 lire per month, with the prize money doubled in the event of victory. After two such victories, at Piacenza and Crema, Alberto suffered a typically spectacular accident on the Padua circuit when a rear tyre burst and he was catapulted from the saddle of a wild Bianchi for some 20 yards, fortunately coming to land in the leafy branches of a plane tree!

1939 saw his first victory abroad and his last victory on two wheels, winning the Gold Medal in the very tough Salzburg Six Days' Trial, disputed in the Tirolean zone of GarmischPartenkirken. Comparisons between father and son were starting to become irresistible.

Accordingly, this year saw Alberto become increasingly keen to transfer his abilities from two to four wheels - and race motor cars, just as his father, Antonio, had done. He had actually learnt to drive a car by buying a Fiat "Balilla". The man who was to give him the chance of changeover, had been an old friend of Antonio Ascari. His name: Enzo Ferrari, now 42 years old

Back in 1932, Alfa Romeo had temporarily abandoned its own racing activities, and handed their P3 cars over to Enzo Ferrari, who formed a very successful racing team, calling it "Scuderia Ferrari". Giulio Ramponi, Antonio's former mechanic, was a member of Ferrari's first-rate technical staff. Then in 1937, Ferrari had disbanded his Scuderia and made a complete break with Alfa-Romeo. For he wanted to realize a dream of his own.

Using Fiat parts, Ferrari now prepared two 8-cylinder 1500 c.c. sportscars at his Modena workshops, calling them the

"815" and entered them for the 1940 Mille Miglia race, to be held on a closed circuit in the triangle Brescia Mantua Cremona, as the Brescia Grand Prix. For his drivers, Enzo chose a fairly experienced driver, the Marquis Lotario Rangoni - and the 22 year-old Alberto (exactly the same age as Antonio when he entered his first motorcar race), whose potential, he felt,was clearly evident from his motorcycle successes.

The race took place in the Spring of 1940. Although it would have been good to have his father's old mechanic Giulio Ramponi at his side on that first race, Giulio was otherwise employed in England. So it was his cousin, Giovanni Minozzi, experienced Alfa-Romeo driver, who sat in the cockpit beside him on the starting line. His close motorcycle racing friend, Silvio Vailati, who had given valuable pre-race help and encouragement, was the last to wish his determined pal luck.

The Ferrari 815s were up against Lancias, Alfa-Romeos, Fiats and above all, a German team of five, 2-liter BMWs, with fully enclosed aerodynamic body; but Alberto was determined to show the Nazi sportsmen just what an Ascari was made of.

After a furious and impetuous start, in which he was leading the Marquis of Rangoni by almost a minute, and the rest of the 1.5 liter class competitors by even more, the Ferrari 815 could not stand up to the foolhardy pace forced on it, and very soon after the first 90-odd mile lap, a valve broke and Ascari had to retire. Rangoni's car also retired soon after. The Germans won and Enzo Ferrari decided to go back to the drawing board. For Alberto, failure was lightened by a crucial realization; he had actually raced a car along the same Cremona Straight with the self-same energy of style as his father had done some sixteen and seventeen years before. There were even some who, becoming nostalgic over the name "Ascari" prophesied a brilliant future for him - among them a melancholy 48 year-old spectator, sitting in the Grandstand at Grazie in Mantua, the legendary Tazio Nuvolari, who, when himself a young man, had been allowed a drive in an Alfa-Romeo, by the great Antonio Ascari himself.

It was during that first half of 1940, that Alberto Ascari came to meet three people who were each, in their own way, to play extremely significant roles in the rest of his life: Gigi Villoresi;

Nino Farina; and Mietta Tavola.

"A Second Shadow?"

"Papa died never having driven a motor car." So recalls Luigi ("Gigi") Villoresi, born in Milan in 1909. "But in 1917 he purchased a motor car, and Andrea our chauffeur soon found it impossible to stop either me, or my three brothers, Eugenio, Pino and Emilio ("Mimi") or my sister, Rosy, from learning to drive at a very early age. We developed a passion for motoring, which soon progressed to Sunday races around impossible mountain roads. The first to race was my elder brother Eugenio, but after he had crashed into a river, he decided to stop!"

"My first race was a hillclimb. I drove Papa's Ansaldo Berlina - 5 meters long, 6-cylinders of engine, 7 seats - a monstrous, ludicrous machine. But with my brother Mimi as mechanic, we won that race, and a magnificent gold watch as a prize.

"Our first *real* racing car was a Fiat Balilla 1500 sportscar, with which Mimi and I drove in the 1928 Mille Miglia and the 1933 Monte Carlo Rally. Then in 1935, I bought a 4-cylinder second-hand Maserati and took part in the Monte Carlo Grand Prix with our chauffeur as mechanic; rather inexperienced, we did not perform very well! Two years later, in 1937, I purchased a brand new Maserati for 75,000 lire. Then with three friends - Count Gianni Lurani, Franco Cortese and Enrico Minetti - we created the "Scuderia Ambrosiana", each one having his own mechanic and complete with Secretary/ President, Signor Possani.

"At the end of 1937, as I had known Achille Varzi, I received a thrilling telegram from the Maserati brothers, saying, 'At Livorno Grand Prix, there's a car ready at your disposal.'

"In the meantime, my younger brother Mimi, who had raced two or three times in my first Maserati, including his Milan Circuit victory, had been offered by Enzo Ferrari, the chance to race an Alfa-Romeo for the Scuderia Ferrari.

"With the result that at the Livorno Grand Prix, I, driving a

Maserati, duelled against my brother Mimi Villoresi in an Alfa-Romeo. We took it in turns for 1st and 2nd place. Our older brother, Eugenio, looking for a better view had gone to a famous corner, climbed up into a tree and perched himself on a branch overhanging the track; he became so taken by the excitement of watching his two brothers, that the branch broke and he fell off!

"Mimi won the race, because I retired with mechanical trouble. But we celebrated this victory together. Fifteen days later, there was a magnificent race at Pescara Alfa-Romeo, Maserati, Mercedes and Auto-Union. At a certain point, Count Trossi, driving an 8-cylinder Maserati, came into the pits, obviously tired. Alfieri Maserati, one of the two brothers said,

'Gigi, you try it!'

'But I've never driven this car before - you're asking me to go from a 180 h.p. engine up to 350 h.p. - '

'Yes or No?'

"So I drove off, and it went fantastically, so much so that I broke the track record! Then I was stopped, because Count Trossi had regained his confidence. But it was a fabulous thing to happen that an Italian car, driven by a 29 year-old unknown, had beaten the might of Mercedes and Auto-Union, driven by Caracciola, Varzi and Nuvolari."

Towards the end of 1939, tragedy hit the Villoresi family. "Mimi" was killed while testing an experimental Alfa-Romeo around Monza Autodrome - just after the Loggia Curve.

"We'll never know what happened. They told me he was not well. I don't believe that. What is certain is that my brother had no life insurance, and he had to be insured. The Villoresi family have never asked Ferrari for a penny. To obtain 'cover' for him, we had to know what was under the bonnet of that Alfa. But they would not tell us. The car went off and Emilio was killed. After that, for some time, my opinion of Enzo Ferrari dropped very low. I lost my sympathy for him.

"Fifteen days after the tragedy, there was an important race at Abbazia. Emilio's death had been a great blow to my mother. She said nothing to me but I knew she wanted me to stop. The Maserati brothers, with understanding, advised me not to race. Instead I went, because I had no choice. Either I overcame the traumatic reaction immediately or for me, motor racing was finished. That day, I raced with a terrible fury in my body - and won. For both my brother and myself.

"In fact, we always did things for ourselves, *not* for the public. We raced for an intimate pleasure and sensation, but always with a sense of responsibility to whoever had put the car at our disposal, even if this responsibility was not always reciprocated. Until the last day I raced, I always kept this in mind. It was passion which made us race. People say that, knowing the risks, a race-driver is a madman. They are not altogether wrong, except that deep down those risks are calculated ones. But the passion made us forget them!

"In the Spring of 1940," Gigi continues, "I do not recall the exact date, I was approached by a young man who wanted to buy an Alfa-Romeo. I persuaded him that it would be better for him to buy Maserati, a 1.5 liter 6-cylinder supercharged single seater model, which I would let him have for 12,000 lire. He told me he could just about afford this figure because another racing driver, Piero Taruffi, had agreed to come in with him on the deal. What he did *not* know was that I had bought this Maserati only hours before at Pavia, and that the front of the engine was still hot from welding!

"But it was too late. He had bought the car. Thus my first impression of this young man, and his of me, were not exactly favorable. His name was Alberto Ascari."

With a keen desire to receive his Grand Prix baptism, he took that Maserati to the Starting Line of the Tripoli Grand Prix in Libya, North Africa. Although the Germans were too busy to appear, Alfa-Romeo turned up in force with their powerful 158 cars. Among their drivers, a Dr. Giuseppe ("Nino") Farina, twelve years older than Alberto. It was against this doctor that Alberto was to struggle across the Grand Prix circuits of Europe, for post-war honors.

Giuseppe Farina was born in 1906, on the same day as his father, Giovanni, and his Uncle Pinin had opened their motorbody building coachworks in Turin. Like Alberto Ascari, his childhood was spent in the atmosphere of motor cars. Farina's first race was with his father in the Aosta - Gran

San Bernardo hillclimb of 1925, and it proved his first accident, because he broke his collar-bone, an injury he managed at
frequent intervals during his career. Returning to racing in 1933
at Livorno, he drove a Siata 509 in a race where the Cup had been
presented by arch-Fascist Count Galeazzo Ciano. In 1934, he
was recruited to drive Alfa-Romeos for the Scuderia Ferrari, and
during the next five years, this young Doctor of Political Science
(not of Medicine), an admirer and friend of the great Nuvolari,
showed a fierce exuberance, echoed in a style of driving that was
confused, violent, and sometimes dangerously decisive and
aggressive. Although this approach won him the Championship
of Italy in 1937, his uncompromising , instinctively egotistical,
imperious style of driving was often carried out at the expense of
others.

Of the 1939, Tripoli Grand Prix, Gigi Villoresi has recalled: "It
was run on the new $1\frac{1}{2}$ liter Formula. Mercedes had prepared a
$1\frac{1}{2}$ liter car. I had a $1\frac{1}{2}$ liter Maserati with double supercharger,
and there was the entire Alfa-Romeo team. The Alfetta 158 had a
higher speed, but my car was faster in acceleration. In practice, I
did a record lap, but unfortunately on the day of the race, the
'Ghibli' arrived, that notorious heat-wave from the desert,
creating a temperature of 45°C - a terrible experience! With their
technical expertise, the Germans had modified their 'plumbing'
as well as their oil and fuel mixtures. With the result that during
the race, while the Maseratis and Alfa-Romeo's blew up from
overheating, Hermann Lang won in the Mercedes.

"Now on the Mellaha circuit, before arriving at the
Grandstand, there was a long straight, then in front of the
Grandstand, a slight bend, which if you didn't want to end up in
the sand , you had to take in 3rd gear with a certain acceleration.
On this curve, Nino Farina, in his attempt to get the Grandstand
crowd to cheer him on, passed by in such a way, that on at least
four or five occasions, I was nearly forced off the track. This was
a characteristic of Farina."

One year later, Farina won the 1940 Tripoli Grand Prix, with
Alberto Ascari coming 9th overall and 3rd in his Class. But that
race taught Alberto a great deal. Journalists and doyens
remarked on "an easy style, controlled, without cunning,
reflexes apparent - all qualities not easy to find in a man as young

as Ascari."

Although one of the ace-motorcyclists required by the Militia Stradale (Road Police), Alberto had realized early that one of Italy's major theaters of war, when Mussolini, "Il Duce", came to officially announce his country's entry, would be North Africa. He consequently decided to team up together with his uncle, and also with Gigi Villoresi in the business of exporting oil and transport vehicles down through the Peninsula across the Mediterranean to North Africa. This partnership at once brought him into the Villoresi household.

During the late 1930's, the law of "Casa Villoresi" in Corso Vercelli, near Via Washington, had been one of freedom and happiness, always full of friends, with parties and dances and dinner parties. Among that happy circle were two, attractive blondes, the Tavola sisters. Maria Antonietta ("Mietta") Tavola had been a very close friend of "Mimi" Villoresi, and much affected when he was killed.

Mietta was now introduced to Gigi's new business partner - Alberto Ascari. He was a year younger than her and was surprised, almost offended to discover that this Milanese girl had never heard of Antonio Ascari, his great racing driver father. But before long, Mietta had realized Alberto's immense filial affection and hero-worship for his father.

Although Alberto could not dance when they first met, as Mietta later recalled: "He came one evening and said 'Let's dance!' and I saw that he suddenly knew how to dance. After a while, I asked him, and he confided in me that he had secretly gone to a dance school so as to be able to go out dancing with me, to please me! Before long, we had fallen in love."

Italy's last motor-race before she entered the war was the Targa Florio, held that year in Palermo along the lanes of the Favourita Park, on May 23rd. Alberto's over-eagerness to win, only threw him off course, seriously damaging the Maserati. The winner was Gigi Villoresi.

Three days later, as Mietta has recalled, "He told me that he was going with some friends to Genoa to see a motorcycle race. 'But by 7 o'clock I'll be back home and I'll telephone you' he said. Well, 7 o'clock, 8 o'clock, 9 o'clock all passed, without a sound. As his friend was engaged to a Genoa girl, I thought they must have invited him out for a meal. Annoyed, I telephoned my sister, and that evening, I went out with her and two boyfriends instead. He returned that evening very late and passed in front of my house. . . 'I went out because you never bothered to telephone me' I remonstrated with him. 'I never bothered to telephone you, because my friend was killed in the motorcycle race,' he replied, deathly pale."

Alberto's friend, probably his closest, was Silvio Vailati. The race was Italy's final pre-war motorcycle contest, the Circuit of Corso Italia at Genoa. The date was May 26 - the same "month-day" on which Antonio Ascari had lost his life, also in a race, some 15 years before.

15 days later, Italy entered the War.

"A Gift Of Nature"

During the War, the Ascari-Villoresi transport agency did not exactly flourish - for at the back of both Alberto and Gigi's minds was that magic phrase - "When this War is over, back to motor-racing!"

One example of the success of their operation, was a batch of lorries to be shipped over to Tripoli. when they were about to embark, Alberto, extremely lovesick for Mietta, and not totally involved in his work, decided to return to Milan, leaving Gigi to make the voyage on his own. Just before the transport ship reached Tripoli, it capsized. Fortunately everyone in the water was equipped with ship's whistles, which they proceeded to blow until they were rescued, including Villoresi. Alberto arrived back at Milan totally ignorant of this ludicrous disaster!

In December, 1941, Mietta Tavola became pregnant, and on January 22 1942, the couple who had first met on the 2nd of the month, were married at the Basilica of Sant Ambrogio. Gigi Villoresi was a witness. The child was born on August 2 1942, a boy named Antonio ("Tonino") after his grandfather.

Fortunately, because of his oil supply business to the Italian Army, Alberto was never called up, but he became perhaps overwary of the possibility that, should the Germans ever catch up with him, they would take him back to Germany. One summer, he and Mietta were at the countryside resort of Col Maiur, in the Val d'Aosta on the Italian/French/Swiss frontiers. Mietta has recalled: "One evening, in the hotel, we heard the noise of lorries going by. We went to the windows, and there were German troops. So all those men who could have been recruited, ran off into the woods, and stayed in hiding for over a week, until the Germans moved on. In the evening, I would go into the woods to take Alberto something to eat -very romantic!"

At the cessation of hostilities, Alberto was 27 years-old, a calm and apparently contented married man, plumper for eating his wife's well cooked pasta, planning to put his father's old car agency business back on its feet again, and to give his mother, Signora Eliza, as peaceful an old age as possible. Such a bourgeois life would appear to have excluded his participation in motor racing. Indeed, up until July 25 1946, when their second child, Patrizia was born, Alberto told Mietta that when he went to a motor race he was merely there to watch their mutual friend Gigi competing and sometimes winning - for example, the Nice Grand Prix and the Voghera Circuit. But one day, Alberto went to see Gigi race in Mantua. Before the race, instead of sitting in the Grandstand, he climbed behind the steering wheel of Gigi's Maserati - and reflected. From that moment, he decided to resume his career.

Gigi recalls: "Without telling his wife, he raced my Maserati round the Princess of Piedmont's Circuit in Naples. There, immediately in evidence, was his innate ability to become a great race driver.

"In my opinion, great singers are born with their voice, and then they perfect it every day with ten hours of practice. In the same way, a champion race driver is born with this Gift of Nature, which is then refined with craft and practice. All you can learn is skill, but skill cannot make a real champion. A champion is someone with something extraordinary - a flair, a sixth sense - a touch of madness. There's no other way."

Following further clandestine practice up at Monza, Alberto Ascari's first official chance, taken with the knowledge of, but against the will of both his wife and his mother came in Egypt in March 1947 at the International Grand Prix. It was an extraordinary affair, organized by Piero Dusio.

During the War, Piero Dusio, a wealthy merchant, had said to Engineer Giaccosa, Fiat's Designer at Turin, "I would like a small, single-seater racing car that can be mass-produced." With Fiat's permission, Giaccosa designed the 1100 c.c. 55 h.p. Cisitalia and some 50 cars were mass-produced. So in March 1947, a fleet of Cisitalias was despatched to Cairo, together with a group of experienced Italian drivers, including Piero Dusio himself, Basadonna, Ghersi, de Sauge, Lurani - and Alberto. Louis Chiron was also there from France.

So that no favoritism should be suspected and to avoid

jealousy these drivers drew lots for their cars. The contest took place not far from the gaze of the sphynx on March 9 in the gardens of El Ghezira, a residential quarter of Cairo, situated on a little island in the River Nile - round a 1½km circuit with numerous twisting little curves.

Alberto shared the same bedroom as Serafini. both having known one another from pre-War motorcycle racing days. The night before the race, Corado Milanta, a photo-journalist who was to become great friends with Alberto, told him: "Remember that you have a name which is like a blank cheque, because you are an Ascari and you have a responsibility."

Alberto, wearing his old Bianchi helmet came 2nd in his heat, while Serafini, wearing his old Gilera helmet, came 3rd. In the Final, Taruffi shot into the lead, pursued by Cortese, Dusio and Ascari, who for 10 laps struggled to get into 3rd position by overtaking Dusio. On the 11th lap, he was successful in overtaking him, and went off in pursuit of the leader, Franco Cortese - only to come 2nd, 13 seconds behind him. King Farouk presented a gold cup to the winner - and the group of Italians returned home the best of friends.

Although the race had only been watched by a few desultory Egyptians sitting in the upper seats of the empty Grandstand, encouraged by his near victory, and by being acclaimed by the Italian Press as "Il nuovo astro" (the new star), Alberto now definitely decided to continue his motor-racing career in earnest. Three months later he decided to team up with Gigi.

In the years that were to follow, Gigi Villoresi and Alberto Ascari were to become one of the most famous duos in motor racing history. It became one of the most famous master-protégé combinations in sporting history, one where the pupil eventually completely outshone the teacher. Using his pre-War years of motor-racing experience, Gigi taught Alberto all the tricks of the game, gave him supreme confidence and impressed on him the need for absolute discipline. And Alberto, intensely serious, was to train assiduously for hour after hour, under Gigi's watching eye.

"Above all," Gigi has recalled, "when we were practicing before a race - he put himself behind me to see how I placed myself for the corners. One can have this gift, but skill one learns by racing. Take cornering, where one curve requires you to take an angle of incidence different from another curve. One is not so much interested in entering it fast, but in *leaving* it fast. Such things I taught to Alberto - respect for the engine, its mechanics. Often we chatted and exchanged just about every idea that can be exchanged.

"It was very strange that between two race drivers - such a friendship *could* exist - but this for us was a friendship outside racing. Up until the starter's flag, we were the greatest friends in the world, each one with scruples as regards the other. But during the race, both of us did everything in our power to beat the other. Whoever won, did so because he had performed better. We existed on this single principle: whoever was in the lead after 40 laps of a 50 lap race must be left alone. We did this because it was stupid to flog the two cars; better to respect them."

Maseratis of Modena had been the first Italian car company to get back into racing after the War by digging out some of their pre-War cars. In 1947, the Maserati brothers left the company and their partners, the Orsi family was left with a free-hand. From the enthusiasm of the persuasive, accommodating Omer Orsi, came their first Grand Prix car - the tubular-framed 16 valve Maserati - the 4 CLT.

To buy one of these cost Alberto five million lire, of which he had to scrape together three million in ready cash and the remainder in IOU. In this he was helped out by Gigi.

Now a member of the 'Scuderia Ambrosiana,' together with Villoresi, Ascari went to France, 22 years after Antonio's fateful Grand Prix at Montlhéry - and once again an Ascari raced on French soil in the Marne Grand Prix at Rheims. Alberto upheld the family name admirably, getting up into second place in a field studded with aces of the Villoresi, Sommer, Chiron caliber - until, as Alberto later recalled: "The engine blew up - indeed everything that could blow up, blew up! For a time, still in debt to Maseratis, I wasn't sure whether to go off and join the Foreign Legion or to strip down the Maserati piece by piece, and rebuild it. I chose the second solution even though it seemed to me the *least* logical at the time."

Whilst his Maserati was in a state of disrepair, Alberto lost no time, and borrowed Minetti's Maserati, to race at the Albi Grand Prix on July 13, no less, coming in 5th.

His own Maserati now ready, Alberto and Gigi went together to the Nice Grand Prix, where, racing with an already improving style, he struggled with the great French ace, Jean Pierre Wimille on a Simca Gordini, for 2nd place, but had to stop at the pits on lap 72 with gearbox trouble - Villoresi winning the race, Ascari placed 4th.

In September, this 29 year-old from Milan raced on his home ground - on the Fiera Circuit of Milan (Monza Autodrome was being repaired after wartime damage) - up against a pack of four powerful Alfa-Romeo 158s. On a $3\frac{1}{2}$Km circuit to be rounded 100 times, he would be watched by a vast number of spectators, fully expectant that despite the odds, a Milanese with the name "Ascari" had to win. In his attempt to do battle with these Alfa-Romeo's, for fourteen of those laps, Alberto engaged in furious combat with his fellow citizen Sanesi on the Alfa - and did so in such an apparently determined way, that the crowd soon began to cheer him. As they cheered, a word came to be heard above all others: "Ciccio! Ciccio! Ciccio!"

For the Milan crowd had found an affectionate nickname for their new hero, Alberto Ascari. It was a nickname they were to chant ever louder during the next eight years as he became their idol. "Ciccio" means, literally, "Chubby" or "Tubby"

At the end of that race, "Ciccio" Ascari finished 5th, despite broken fuel tank straps and the loss of his exhaust pipe, but having made the sparks fly at the shoulders of those four Alfas. Gigi Villoresi, who despite his having driven a new two-stage supercharged Maserati, had been beaten by his pupil, could still be pleased with his pupil's progress.

Three week's later, the pair of them went to the Modena Circuit - this time Alberto was racing a new 6-cylinder 2000 Maserati sportscar, the A6G, instead of his temperamental GP model. Following the course as it wound through the streets of a city never designed for the motor car, by Lap 24 Alberto was in the lead. But then Giovanni Bracco, driving a 3 liter Delage, swerved to miss a stationary Ferrari and left the road, injuring many spectators, some fatally. The organizers, flagged in all the remaining cars and stopped the race, declaring as winner whoever happened to be in the lead at that time. The date was September 28 1947. Alberto Ascari had scored his first victory on four wheels, without even finishing the race. Gigi Villoresi came a close 2nd.

Although he retired with mechanical troubles in races at Losanna and Turin, by this time Alberto had had another meeting with Omer Orsi of Maserati.

"It was easy to agree with Orsi that he was having to consign a car to a hasty client. But I gave him my reconstructed GP Maserati in exchange for a brand new, flame red model, to be ready in three months for the 1948 Season. In the meantime, I felt it important to assure him that I would pay all the IOU's, from the first to the last, without asking for one day's postponement.

"Thus I remained for three months, without a car, so as to avoid the "Foreign Legion" alternative."

"Eclipsing The Shadows"

In the opinion of some scholars, the black cat is the creature of a Black Witch and therefore if it crosses your path, you will be unlucky. Two events at the beginning of 1948 were to give Alberto Ascari a religious horror of black cats.

On the morning of April 1st, he was driving his Maserati sportscar out of the garage to go to the Circuit of Sicily race, when a black cat placed itself in front of his path. He braked, sounded his horn and the cat raced off in fear. During the 620-mile race around Sicily's mountainous and hairpin-infested coast "everything that could happen to me, *did* happen; first of all I left the track, fortunately without serious consequences; then I burnt out the 'Delco'; then the rear axle broke. My mechanic fell ill and was sick. Finally, before I arrived at Palermo, the car made a sudden leap and stopped. I opened the bonnet; there was a rag caught round the engine!'

"One month later, I was going towards the Starting Line at the depart of the Mille Miglia race at Brescia, when a large tom-cat cut across my path. I was irritated and left reluctantly. For a time we were in the lead. Then at Rimini, it became difficult to change gear; the stick was stiff. To make it work, I had to use both hands. Each time I had to change speeds whilst turning or on a dangerous stretch, the maneuver became a nightmare. The mechanic and I were in despair. We pushed on somehow or other as far as Monsummano, but there, a connecting-rod melted and we had to retire." As we shall see, in the years that followed, Alberto was to take this cat superstition to extremes.

On May 16 1948, the Monaco Grand Prix was re-established after a ten year break in its own history. This was a glamorous race, surrounded by the atmosphere of a harbor of luxury yachts, surrounded by luxury hotels and flats and a Casino, nestling in the mountains of a principality of its own. Still waiting for his new Maserati, Alberto raced his 1947 model, whilst Gigi was again at the wheel of his two-stage super-charged version. Doctor Farina was also driving a Maserati, the very latest model, in the absence of any Alfa-Romeos, and it was Dr. Farina who won the race, with one minute's lead after 100 laps at 60 m.p.h. in just over $3\frac{1}{4}$ hours. In a testing race, where only 8 out of the 21 cars finished, Alberto first suffered gear-trouble and fell from 4th to 12th place, then later the oil pump failed and he had to retire. But at quarter distance, he took over Gigi's sick Maserati (it had only 3rd gear left!) and was able to nurse a smoking car over the finishing line, officially placed 5th, although in reality 4th, the judges having mistakenly declared Trintignant in that position. Following two further retirements - at Bari and Mantua Alberto finally came into possession of his own 4CLT/48 Formula One Grand Prix Maserati, capable with supercharger of 300 h.p. in fact, lower, faster and more reliable. For its first public appearance, he took it to San Remo, just across the border from Monte Carlo, where on the newly opened Ospedaletti Circuit, the Italian "round-the-houses" equivalent of the Monaco Grand Prix, the contest was held through the streets of two villages and out into the countryside behind them.

The race was a Maserati benefit - a three-cornered fight between Ascari, Villoresi and Farina, each leading in turn. Then Farina retired and Ascari the pupil, led Villoresi the teacher, over the line, coming in at the end, with his seat and cockpit full of tarry gravel, showing the conditions under which he won. He had covered the 170 odd miles/85 laps in three hours 3 minutes. at an average 57.66 m.p.h. But more important as a top class driver, he had definitely "arrived". Thereafter, the 4 CLT/48 Maserati became known as the "San Remo Maserati".

The European Grand Prix on the tricky Bremgarten circuit at Berne, Switzerland, was a tragic event, because in practice the legendary Italian driver, Achille Varzi, Nuvolari's great rival - and also Omobono Tenni, were killed. Then, in the race itself, where Villoresi came 3rd and Alberto 5th, the pre-War official Auto-Union driver, Christian Kautz also lost his life. Soon after, at the House of Portello, Alfa-Romeo learnt that their other driver, Felice Trossi, was suffering from an incurable illness and were forced to retire.

Two weeks later, on Sunday July 18, the 35th French Grand Prix was held at Rheims. It was twenty-three years, to the month, that Antonio Ascari had lost his life, driving an Alfa-Romeo in the French Grand Prix. Alberto was aware of number-coincidences. Alberto agreed to drive - for the first and last time in his life a 1 liter supercharged Grand Prix *Alfa-Romeo* 158 in this race - but not without an endless debate en route to the race with Gigi, whose brother had also been killed in an Alfa Romeo. If Gigi had entered a Maserati, why then did not Alberto stay with *his* Maserati? As they say in Milan, "La minestra riscaldata non piace" - "re-heated minestrone is not appealing."

What is even stranger is that when he turned up on the Starting Grid at Rheims, Alberto Ascari's car bore the Racing Number 26 - the date-day of the deaths of both his father and of his friend, Silvio Vailati. Just how far could he tempt Fate? The race proved undramatic, remote-controlled. As team-mate to Wimille and Sanesi - and as their junior, he was expected to let them win. Indeed, every time Jean Pierre Wimille came into the pits, Alberto went into 1st position, averaging around 105 m.p.h., but then deliberately took his foot off the accelerator to allow the famous Frenchman back into the lead. So also with Sanesi, whom Alberto also allowed to pass him for 2nd place on Lap 55, again in accordance with pit signals. Thus, showing a superb control that his father simply could not have brooked, Alberto Ascari was placed 3rd, behind Wimille and Sanesi, having also made a daring attempt to lay a ghost which must have been haunting him. But had he, in fact, laid it? During the rest of his career, Alberto was never able to bring himself to race at Montlhéry. . .

Pescara, on the Adriatic, with its 17-mile circuit, was the next venue for the Ascari/Villoresi duo - both in Maserati sportscars. It was a fast circuit and to be lapped in sizzling hot August conditions. It comprised two long straights and the third leg up the triangle up into the mountains and a straggling village.

Alberto came to the Starting Line with a big bandage on his

51

nose, signs of a road accident suffered a week before. On the third lap, the Maserati's suspension went and he had to retire, standing in the pits, arms folded, a spectator, watching the other cars racing along the Montesilvano Straight.

But then, unexpectedly, poor Giovanni Bracco, came into the pits, totally unnerved, still haunted by the nightmare deaths he had caused at Modena, and abandoned his A6G Maserati car Number 8 in perfect working order, right in front of Alberto.

Seeing his chance, Alberto at once climbed into Bracco's car and went off in pursuit of Sommer and Villoresi. On Lap 10 he came into refuel in such haste that they almost set light to his car, then was off again. Six laps later, first Villoresi, then Sommer, retired, leaving the road clear for an Ascari walkover. Just managing to avoid ending up in a ditch on one of his last laps, Alberto scored a memorable victory that day, averaging 83 m.p.h. and some 11 minutes ahead of 2nd placed Count Sterzi.

The Italian Grand Prix, contested on the circuit of the Valentino Public Park, saw Wimille lst, Villoresi 2nd, Sommer 3rd and Ascari 4th. But behind that statement is the fact that, badly held back at the Start, Alberto pulled himself up into that 4th place, by driving his GP Maserati for some 186 miles in the rain, *minus goggles or vizor!*

That October, the first post-War British Grand Prix was held on a somewhat featureless wartime airfield called Silverstone, not far from Northampton in the English Midlands. Alberto and Gigi drove night and day to reach the 3.8 mile circuit and their 4 CLT/48 cars, ably prepared by Maserati's Chief Mechanic, Guerrino Bertocchi. They arrived only just in time to put in four laps of unofficial practice, during which Alberto made the fastest lap of any competitor, so that both he and Gigi were put at the back of the Grid for the Start.

Watched by an estimated 100,000 spectators, this turned out to be a Maserati benefit. After only 3 laps, Villoresi led Ascari with Reg Parnell and Prince Birabongse - also in GP Maseratis - a long way behind with the rest of the pack. Alberto's 4th Lap was a track record of 76.12 m.p.h. which Gigi was to beat later on by 0.5 m.p.h.

The race was one where teacher and pupil played at passing and re-passing each other. Ascari led at 20 laps, Villoresi at Lap 30. Ascari used his brakes harder than Villoresi and had to come in for a wheel change; losing his exhaust pipe also did not deter him. Soon after Lap 50 Villoresi could no longer read his revs, the rev-counter having shaken itself out of the dashboard and fallen down, lodging under the clutch pedal denying Gigi even a clutch, so that he had to be more careful with his gear-changing. Thereafter, Gigi's lead on Alberto dropped so that at the end of the race, he was only 14 seconds ahead of his pupil, both of them having averaged 72 m.p.h.

Following the checkered flag, a huge crowd of enthusiastic spectators swarmed across the track towards the drivers and their cars in the pits and would have mobbed the Italian winners, had not Alberto and Gigi slipped out the back to their sportscar and made a hasty retreat across a potato field, thus rendering the prize-giving ceremony an impossibility!

Driving back towards Italy, Alberto Ascari decided that despite "English jelly" and the food rationing - he rather liked the friendliness of the English, their way of life and their beautiful countryside. In the years to come, the English came to admire Alberto Ascari, almost as much as his native Italians.

Just over a fortnight later, the inseparable pair took their two Maseratis to Monza Autodrome, which had just been rebuilt with incredible speed in one hundred days - the track having been completely re-made and the corners widened so as to make it even faster.

Here was contested the Apertura (Opening) Grand Prix, following a gigantic parade round the circuit, which saw even Tazio Nuvolari take part.

At the race, won by four Alfa-Romeo's with Alberto hot in pursuit and placed 5th, Signor Gallo, President of Alfa-Romeo, fully realizing that Ascari was now a name to be reckoned with and only bound to improve, commented, "He is a driver I would very much like to have."

Gallo's dream would never come true. For at the end of that year, "Scuderia Ferrari" had been reborn at Modena in the shape of the Ferrari Type 125, co-designed by the brilliant

Gioacchino Colombo. And Enzo Ferrari, was already scheming that two works drivers from Maserati's 'Scuderia Ambrosiana' might leave Omer Orsi and come and drive cars for him. Those two drivers were, of course, Villoresi and Ascari, who were, according to the Championship of Italy result that year, two out of the top three Italian motor-racing drivers; the third was Dr. Giuseppe Farina.

"Enter Fangio"

"When I began to hear people talking about this 'Fangio' coming over from Argentina, I was afraid. I was afraid of this foreigner, and that Alberto was going to have to take many more risks just to overtake him." (Mietta Ascari)

In 1949, an Italian called Alberto Ascari went to race in South America, and an Argentinian called Juan Manuel Fangio came to race in Europe.

Fangio, seven years older than Alberto, had learned to drive cars in competition on dirt-tracks and in gruelling long distance road races, lasting many dusty days and covering thousands of miles of rough Latin American terrain. He achieved his first great victory, the International Grand Prix of the North, driving a 6-cylinder Chevrolet Coupé in 1940, aged 29.

Eight years later, a number of European drivers went to Argentina for the winter races, among them Jean-Pierre Wimille who immediately saw Fangio's talent and offered him a drive in one of the spare Maseratis they had brought over from Europe. It was a chance he had been waiting for. Later that year, in Paris, the unknown Fangio was hosted by Wimille.

In January 1949, as part of the "Temporada", a race was organized at Palmero Park between the town of Buenos Aires and the River Plate, for a cup donated and to be presented by President Juan Domingo Peron of the Argentine Republic. Among those entered - the "Old Guard" of Wimille, Villoresi and Farina, then Fangio and Ascari both on 4 CLT Maseratis as the promising newcomers.

The evening before practice, Carlo Pintacuda, a great sportscar driver living in Buenos Aires, invited all the drivers Wimille, Fangio, Gordini, Filippini, Villoresi - 'and Alberto Ascari - to a meal at his home. Gigi recalls: "When we sat down to eat, Pintacuda, extremely superstitious, realized that we were 13 at the table. There was a frozen, pregnant silence! Now in that house there was a little 5 year old urchin, fast asleep. She was immediately woken up, and, bawling her head off, brought to the table. The following day, Jean Pierre Wimille, the eldest sitting at our dinner table was killed in practice. . ."

Wimille had let his Simca-Gordini car get out of control on a corner and after several somersaults, it crashed into a tree; rumor had it that he found the course blocked by spectators and swerved to avoid them. Wimille died only ten minutes after admission to hospital. Fangio was crestfallen.

The race was watched by a crowd estimated at almost 200,000 spectators, whose proximity to the many-cornered circuit was rather too close for the comfort of any driver, no matter how experienced. It saw the first of many fierce combats to be fought amongst the Villoresi-Farina-Ascari-Fangio quartet. Fangio was the local hero, but the breath-taking and vigorous attacks of young Ascari even won him the wild support of the Argentinians, some of them stepping on the track itself to cheer him on - a hair-raising threat to the driver. Alberto finally won the 1½ hour race at an average 70 m.p.h. beating Gigi by a mere 40 seconds.

On arrival at the Finish, the crowd swarmed hysterically towards Alberto. Fearing that they were going to lynch him for beating their local hero Fangio, he scrambled out of the Maserati and ran for cover. He needn't have done this, for in reality they were going to hoist him shoulder-high in acclaim!

President Peron now proclaimed that the Grand Prix named after his wife, Eva Duarte ("Evita"), would be held in memory of Jean-Pierre Wimille. Taking place one week later, it was spoiled by heavy rain, but it was Fangio's chance to get his own back on Ascari. It was a hard-fought battle. Fangio just escaped accident when his Maserati skidded and smote a tree. On Lap 13, Alberto took the lead, Gigi's engine blew up and Dr. Farina also retired with engine trouble. Then with only five laps to go, Alberto had to retire so as to avoid a potential fire when his exhaust pipe came away. Argentinian Oscar Galvez went into the lead at the wheel of a 3.8 liter Alfa to win the race with Fangio on his tail.

Following Dr. Farina's victory in torrential rain at the Rosario GP on February 13, Fangio finally got his own back on February 27 at the unfortunate International Mar del Plata

Grand Prix. In practice Malusardi was involved in a fatal crash in his Maserati, which overturned and caught fire. In the race, Cantoni went off the road into a dense crowd, killing one spectator and injurying eleven. But the race went on. After three pit stops, Alberto gave up with mechanical troubles. Gigi also retired, but not without setting the fastest lap. Following his victory, the Automobile Club of Argentina decided to send their Fangio to Europe with a brand new 4 CLT Maserati.

But before he went, there was one further race to be run against the Villoresi/Ascari/Farina trio - and that was on March 20, in Brazil, at Rio di Janeiro, round the treacherous Gravea circuit, aptly nicknamed the "Devil's Trampoline."

Fangio won. Ascari crashed. He later recalled: "Pulling to the outside to pass a car that was hugging the rails, I collided heavily with another competitor. My Maserati turned a somersault, and a split second later I was lying pinned to the ground, with petrol gushing out of a smashed tank, only centimeters away from me. Fortunately it didn't catch fire. But I cannot remember the scene - for I was knocked unconscious the instant the crash occurred."

As far as injury, he'd gotten off lightly; a fractured collar bone, three broken ribs and three teeth knocked out. He was taken to a hospital for treatment, where, as Gigi remembers, an amusing incident occurred: "When we were travelling from race to race, I was the cashier; it was I who kept the accounts. How at this hospital in Brazil, Alberto was being tended to his every need by this old black nurse. Now Alberto always enjoyed a drink of fresh orange-juice, and eating candies, so one day when I went to visit him, he said 'Gigi, leave me some money to give my nurse for some sweets and drinks?' As I didn't have any small change, I left him some bank-notes.

"But at that stage in his recovery, he saw very little, one eye was completely closed, and the other little better. Later on, when I asked him whether the candies were alright, he said "But Gigi, were you mad? You gave me about 25 thousand lire (about $40) to give to that nurse just to buy something to eat!"

"It is a fact that when Alberto left this hospital, that dear old nurse presented him with a little statue of Santa Lucia, because Santa Lucia is the Saint who heals diseases and injuries to the eyes!" (The Saint's Day of Santa Lucia is December 13.)

During the two months of convalscence, certain changes occurred in European motorsport. Alberto's Argentinian rival, Juan Fangio, nicknamed "El Chueco" because he was slightly bowlegged, had notched up three European race victories in his Maserati - San Remo, Pau and Perpignan. And in the meantime, Commendatore Enzo Ferrari had signed up Villoresi and Ascari as works drivers in his "Scuderia" of the "Cavallino Rampante", (the Prancing Black Horse on a yellow background, formerly symbol of an ace Italian fighter pilot killed in the First World War, who had carried it on the side of his fuselage). The contracts were organized separately, and in rather an oblique sort of manner, that is a story in itself. . .

"The Wizard Of Maranello"

By 1949 Commendatore Enzo Ferrari, 51 years-old, had developed a shrewd ability to recognize and instil his burning passion for motorsport in others. He was a man who, if he wanted to, could make even the kerbstones enthusiastic! "I am not a technician. I am an agitator of men," he once said and on another occasion: "Those close to me, my young drivers, have been lucky enough to have been able to sacrifice themselves for me, which is their duty. And I have the *right* not to thank them." The whim of a Caesar, a magnificent, formidable race manager, who seldom went to see the races in which his cars were being driven, possibly because he was more interested "In setting the fuse, rather than seeing how it would explode" possibly because he no longer wanted to suffer. . .

In 1946, for example, a young 29 year-old designer, called Aurelio Lampredi, with previous experience with the Piaggio aircraft concern, arrived at Ferraris. He was there for six months, but as Lampredi explains: "At Maranello there were certain people, X, Y and Z, including a certain Signor Busso supervising projects, with whom I did not at all get on. So I decided to leave. Ferrari's reaction was 'I'll let you go away, but on condition that when I want you to come back, you must return.' I agreed to sign a pledge to this effect, but added 'This is as much your pledge as mine, Commendatore, because if I return, I do not want Messrs. X, Y or Z to be around.' He agreed, and we both signed.

"After some months, Ferrari telephoned Isotta-Fraschini in Milan, where I was working and said 'Lampredi, you signed a pledge with me, and it's time to respect it.' To which I replied, "Yes, Commendatore, but you have also got a pledge with me.' To which he remarked, 'It is my custom to respect such pledges.' - 'And I don't doubt the fact,' I replied.

'So, tomorrow morning , I'll expect you at Maranello.' So I went, only to learn that he had dismissed X, Y and Z but taken on Engineer Gioacchino Colombo as Consultant. 'You do not know Signor Colombo,' Ferrari said. 'But he is a famous man, and to have a consultant like him is like being invited to a wedding celebration.'

"Colombo would arrive once every fifteen days, whilst I being the sort of person who liked to study my calculations -not to improvize - worked to improve whatever there was, namely the 1500 supercharged car, and we went forward a little.

"About this time, although we had had Nuvolari, Farina, Cortese and Bonetto driving for us, Ferrari decided to take on two official works' drivers - a fairly well known quantity called Villoresi and a lesser known driver, the same age as me, called Ascari. I soon struck up a friendship with both men especially Alberto."

It must have been a remarkable coincidence for Alberto to discover that both his new friend, the designer Aurelio Lampredi, and his wife Mietta, had been born on the *same* year, the *same* month and the *same* day - June 16 1917. As Lampredi comments "I don't know whether I was born two hours before her, or she two hours before me, but we certainly enjoyed some fabulous birthday dinners on that day!"

Alberto Ascari's engagement with Ferrari, who had once raced with his father Antonio, was not as smooth as might have been expected. Corado Milanta has recalled: "In 1948, Felice Bonetto, at Mantua, won a fantastic race, driving a little Cisitalia, against Nuvolari and Cortese in 2-liter Ferraris, Villoresi and Ascari in 2-liter Maseratis; lap by lap, Bonetto overtook each one of these drivers until, by Lap 5, he was leading. After such a beautiful race, Ferrari took on Bonetto.

"Now I used to go up to Modena with Bonetto to chat and eat with Ferrari. Alberto Ascari wanted to drive for Ferrari again, but was not sure whether Ferrari desired it. So Bonetto said 'Leave this one to me'. When Bonetto broached Ferrari, the latter complained, 'That boy gives himself too many airs.' But Bonetto persisted. Eventually Enzo took him on, and in time came to treat Alberto almost like a son."

As for Gigi Villoresi?: "I was in England at a race, when I

received a telegram from Ferrari: 'Villoresi. At Brussels, there is a Formula One car at your disposal. You will find my Agent, Amorotti, at the Hotel X. There is a sportscar race at Luxembourg the week following. We have also sent a car there. If you would like to race it, I shall be pleased. Ferrari.'

"But what in Heaven's name was I going to do? In fact I went to Brussels, won at Brussels, went to Luxembourg, won at Luxembourg - returned to Italy. Alberto, with Corado Filippini, a famous journalist, our most dear friend, with very good relations with Ferrari, suggested I go up there. But I didn't want to go, for I still had little respect for the man. Then one day, I took my car up to Modena, on my own, without Alberto. Ferrari was in bed, indisposed. I went to his bedroom. One, two, three minutes went by. He said nothing. So I said, 'Commendatore, the time has come to speak frankly. I know that between us there is very little rapport. If you intend to discuss doing something, I shall remain. If not, I shall leave.' This speech convinced him. From that moment, in fact, began our collaboration. In the years that followed, I must say that my relationship with Ferrari was of the best; I found him a courteous and a kind person, a great friend."

Villoresi and Ascari were to drive the cars Aurelio Lampredi designed for Ferrari for the next five years, with brilliant and often exciting results.

Alberto's first race appearance in a Formula 2 Ferrari 2000 was on the town circuit of Bari on the Southern Adriatic coast of Italy; after a fierce duel with Villroesi, Bonetto and Landi, he went into a lead that he kept from Lap 40 to 80.

His first race in a Formula One 1 liter supercharged V12 Ferrari followed at the Belgian Grand Prix at Spa-Francorchamps where some 24 years before, his father Antonio had scored such a decisive victory in the P2 Alfa-Romeo. But for Alberto, the son, victory was not yet for the taking at Spa, and he came in 3rd behind Frenchman Rosier and Villoresi.

Imagine the ignominy, one week later, on June 26, when on his home track, Monza Autodrome, he suffered gear trouble on Lap 67 (6 + 7 = 13) and was forced into 3rd place, with a proud Fangio fulfilling a longtime ambition of winning a race on the Italian circuit.

No, Alberto's first victory abroad in a Formula One Ferrari came on July 3, at the Swiss Grand Prix, held on the Bremgarten Circuit at the end of the westbound tram-tracks of the Swiss capital of Berne. Alberto left convinced that he would lose. Several moments before the Start, he had noticed the water in the radiator was leaking into the cylinders. It was clear, in such a situation, that his car would not last the course.

During the race, as if by a miracle, the engine recovered and gave no trouble; Alberto went into a lead that he only lost to Gigi when he stopped to refuel and which he soon regained when Gigi himself stopped to refuel. Alberto came in first after just under 2 hours of driving at an average 90.76 m.p.h., almost a minute ahead of Gigi, thus giving a delighted Enzo Ferrari his first major Grand Prix win.

Exactly two weeks' later, Alberto again took on Fangio at Rheims for the Wimille Cup - Ferrari versus Maserati. After a start with a flooded engine, followed by a rear brake blocking, Alberto made fierce attempts to overtake his Argentinian rival before the latter, retiring with gear trouble, gave his Italian friend the victory he desired at an average 94.7 m.p.h.

Stirling Moss once studied the driving styles of Ascari and Fangio: " I was watching them come round quite a fast, 90 m.p.h. corner, Alberto in the Ferrari would come round and, every time, just touch the straw bales, whilst Fangio in the Alfa Romeo would come round and every time just touch the whisps of straw. The difference between the two men was that Alberto would just kiss the straw bale and Fangio wouldn't quite. I remember thinking, 'How fine a line there is between these two great drivers!"

Exactly two weeks later again, Alberto and Gigi were in Holland, leading again, passing and re-passing each other in the 3rd and final race for the Dutch Grand Prix, held on the 2.7 mile sand-dune circuit of Zandvoort, beside the North Sea, with its sand-dust particles in their noses, in their cockpits and sliding treacherously under the wheels of their Ferraris.

Then there was nearly a nasty accident. On Lap 35, Alberto's front stub-axle snapped! He lost a wheel and instead of crashing into the brick wall of a bridge, fortunately the Ferrari ended up badly damaged against a protective sand barrier. Although Gigi won the race, there was still debate as to whether Alberto might not have re-passed his friend on the last couple of laps, had he not spun off. . .

Switzerland, France, Holland - and next England, back to Silverstone for the "Daily Express" Trophy race. Although it had been rumored they would bring the latest 300 hp-plus two-stage Ferrari, as this was not yet ready, Gigi and Alberto arrived with the well-tried single-stage version, whilst Dr. Giuseppe Farina arrived with one of the six "San Remo" Maseratis, not to mention the four French Lago-Talbots. In the Final, some 23 cars came to the Start, watched by an estimated 100,000 spectators.

Ascari slammed past Prince Birabongse's Maserati on the lst Lap and by Lap 5, Gigi too had climbed up into 2nd place. The Ferraris were working well, separated as they were by 1.2. seconds, a mere car's length, averaging 89.8. m.p.h. This was Grand Prix driving at its best-sprint speeds, brains and cunning evenly matched, hand-to-hand battling by a pupil who was beginning to outshine his teacher.

But now on Lap 15, Dr. Farina's brilliant driving enabled him to pass Gigi and by Lap 19, Ascari led Farina by 0.1. seconds, the Doctor continuing to challenge him. On Lap 20, they sang down the finishing straight side by side. Farina gathered speed on the outside, but Ascari it was who shot his car to take the corner beyond from out of the bend first. Two laps later, the Doctor tried again, almost successfully, but then a newspaper, caught by the wind, wrapped itself round his head and in the confusion of the moment he let his Maserati overslide outwards and bang the straw bales, thus dropping back a vital 10 seconds. Thereafter, Alberto did not relent and crossed the Finishing Line after a race that even he had found really close, followed by an infuriated Farina and a partly satisfied Villoresi.

One week later, the Doctor got his own back with a victory in the Lausanne Grand prix in Switzerland, beating the 'upstart' Alberto, suffering with rear brake and plug problems, by over a minute.

The proverbial fortnight passed again and they were all back at the Monza Autodrome for the final show-down, the Grand Prix of Europe. The only difference was that Ascari and Villoresi were now at the wheels of far more potent, re-designed, double super-charged Ferraris. But then Farina and Taruffi were also at the wheel of two hotted-up Maseratis. The Autodrome, situated in a well-wooded park just outside Monza, in a wide plain, was in track width as broad as a modern trunk road. Its sweeping turns leading into the Finishing Straight were surfaced with stone setts, but the remainder was asphalt. From the Start there was a Kilometer of straight into a vast, sweeping right-hand curve through thickets of trees followed by a winding, very fast section to the far end of the course where two sharp, eased-off right-angles brought the cars back through woodlands to a short straight and a very fast left-hand bend. Here the cars returned parallel with the Finishing Straight and in full view of the huge marble and concrete grandstands, to flash down a Kilometer straight to two stone-paved right angles. These brought them back onto the 2-Kilometer Finishing Straight - allowing them to travel flat out past the Stands. Such a 3.9 mile course, to be completed 80 times, could only fire the ingenuity of a driver or the excitement of many an onlooker, especially if he were Italian.

September 11 was a boiling hot day at Monza. Twenty-four cars, most of them red, glittered on the Starting line. To remind himself of the atmosphere of bygone days, an ageing Tazio Nuvolari stood on that Grid talking to the drivers just before the fall of the Flag. Among them, Alberto Ascari, his face swollen with tooth-ache and his shoes soaked in mineral water to keep them cool.

He shot into a lead that he kept until the end of that almost 3-hour race. He completed his second and fastest lap at 111.14 m.p.h. and continued on superbly, floating through those fast curves with practiced ease and perfect timing. Gigi Villoresi drove in his wheel tracks for 27 laps before retiring with gearbox trouble. Indeed before the race had been going for an hour, all the fastest cars, except "Ciccio" Ascari's, were either blown up or limping round. He was so much in the lead, that he could come in to his pit and spend a leisurely 55 seconds refuelling. changing a plug and taking on oil. He then went off at a slower 105 m.p.h., still leading by 18 seconds, cheered on by an exuberant home crowd, to a glorious Finish, one Lap ahead of Etancelin in 2nd place.

"For me a race is extremely tiring, exhausting," Alberto once explained. "During the race, it is thirst, above all, which torments you - a terrible thirst, which some men must quench during those three hours, thus forfeiting the race. I sweat so profusely in that boiling cockpit, that I sometimes lose as much as 3 to 4 kilos in weight. By the Finish, a bottle of ice-cold mineral water, poured down my throat and down my neck and back, is better than the finest champagne in the world!"

Alberto Ascari had now driven better and faster than his father Antonio *ever* had done. The final achievement for 1949 was yet to come. For on December 18 he was out in the Argentine competing again for General Peron's Cup. And here, despite excessive heat suffered on the soles of his feet, he again succeeded in beating Juan Manuel Fangio on his home territory. Thus at the end of the year, Alberto was European Champion, and also Italian Champion, beating Gigi Villoresi by 340 points and Dr. Farina by 1030.

In the year that was to follow, he was given the chance to go one stage higher - and become motorsport's first World Champion - and failed to achieve this. Why he failed, may be spelt out in two, hyphenated words: Alfa-Romeo.

"The Doctor's Obsession"

The World Championship for motor-racing was launched in 1950. Whoever had amassed enough points by the end of the season would become the first official World Champion.

January found the top drivers back in the Argentine for some Formula 2 races. On January 8 Eva Peron presented Gigi Villoresi with her Trophy, Ascari having spun off course soon after the Start. One week later in the General Martin Grand Prix at Mar del Plata, Ascari beat Farina over the line, Villoresi and Fangio having hit against each other on a bend, both going off course; in the days that followed the Argentine Press accused Villoresi of deliberately effecting this accident so that his friend Alberto could win! The following weekend, Gigi won the Accion de San Lorenzo Grand Prix, Alberto retiring after a newspaper had wrapped itself around the Ferrari's radiator and fouled up the cooling system.

In answer to those Argentine critics, Gigi has explained: "Racing in Argentina during 1949/50, Alberto won two races and I won two races, but it was not because we had a secret agreement to help each other. At Mar del Plata, at the Start, there was Fangio, Farina, Alberto and I. We were racing head-to-tail. There was a section beside the sea, where one could not overtake, and a higher part, 30 meters wide, where one could pass. The good Fangio was undoubtedly a most formidable race-driver but was one who knew his own business. For the first two laps of that race, each time we came to that narrow section, every time I tried to pass, Fangio squeezed me, first to the left, then to the right. On the 3rd lap, I lost my patience, Fangio tried to press me, I held on hard and we left the track together. Alberto won. It was not that I wanted Alberto to win. I did it because I, Villoresi, wanted to win."

A month later, it was raining so heavily at the Start of the

Marseilles Grand Prix, contested at Boreley Park race-course, that the race director advised Villoresi, Ascari and Fangio and the others, "Race wisely for the first lap". Impossible request!

The trio, all on Ferraris, battled together wheel-to-wheel for the whole wet race - passing and re-passing. As they roared down the Finishing Straight on the 80th Lap, Villoresi and Ascari were neck-and-neck - indeed it was a photo-finish with Fangio an extremely close 3rd.

Gigi remembers that, "In the evening, we went to this reception, where there was this strange mayor, who made a tedious, typically French speech, lasting 30 minutes, where he went to the extreme of thanking even the local fire brigade - everyone he could think of! Afterwards, this mayor came up to Alberto and said,

'Monsieur Ascari, as a great sportsman, besides motor racing, what other sports do you enjoy?'

'J'aime beaucoup nager (I like swimming)' said Alberto in his best French. Then to everyone's astonishment, in all innocence, Alberto, who had often gone snow-skiing at Cortina d'Ampezzo since a child, said, 'Et j'aime aussi schier'. Now he *should* have said 'J'aime aussi faire du ski', because 'scier le dos a quelqu'un' means 'to scare the pants off someone' - and even worse - 'chier' pronounced in the same way, means 'to shit'. . .!

Soon after this contest, Alfa-Romeo announced that after one year of inactivity, they were returning to racing with their two-stage, high boost Alfa 158, a much improved and more potent car, and that they had signed up three works drivers - Farina, Fangio, and the experienced Italian veteran, Luigi Fagioli - "the three 'F's". This meant war.

The first battlefield for the Alfa-Ferrari combat was the Ospedaletti Circuit in the San Remo Grand Prix in mid-April. Farina had crashed in practice the day before, so it was up to Fangio to control, for the first time, a powerful car on wet, slippery roads. Fangio made a poor start, sliding about on a very greasy surface, Alberto forging into the lead. But then Alberto spun round and by the time he had sorted himself out, he was 2nd, some 20 seconds behind Fangio - a distance he had only just lessened to 14 seconds when he skidded again and smashed into a wall. Fangio won, and Villoresi, who had also spun round, placed 2nd, but one minute behind.

The second Formula One encounter between the Houses of Portello (Alfa-Romeo) and Maranello (Ferrari) - between Fangio /Farina and Ascari/Villoresi - came one month later, following two Formula 2 and one sportscar victory by Alberto (Modena, Mons and Luxembourg). This was at the Monaco Grand Prix, and involved a multiple pile-up on the first lap, involving half of the nineteen cars.

Farina led the field at the Start, but was soon overtaken by Fangio, followed by Gonzalez, Fagioli, Ascari and the others. Mediterranean wave-tops, carried over the sea-wall by the wind, had been wetting the quayside by the Tabac left-hand corner, and as he came out of that corner, Dr. Farina skidded his Alfa into the wall, bouncing back across the track in the path of the oncoming cars. Villoresi's lightning reactions allowed him to slip past. But thereafter, one car crashed into another and within six seconds, the field was reduced to ten cars. Alberto, also quick to realize the situation, slowed down, threaded his way through and pressed on, having lost valuable seconds.

Meanwhile, Fangio and Villoresi approached for Lap 2. Yellow flags slowed them down to a stop. Fangio filtered through, splashing cautiously through spilled fuel and pressed on to his next circuit. Villoresi also slowed to a halt, but then stalled his engine, falling back into 9th place, then taking the next 12 laps to skillfully climb back up to 3rd place. Alberto also roared off in pursuit of Fangio to a 2nd place that he began to swap with Gigi, passing and re-passing to 2nd and 3rd, despite the irregularly high revs of the Ferrari and a burn on his left foot. When Gigi was forced to retire with rear-axle trouble, Alberto kept that 2nd place to the Finish, despite being lapped by Fangio in the Alfa, while he re-fuelled. In short, it was a resounding victory by Alfa over Ferrari.

Back at Maranello, some radical, behind-the-scenes changes were now made, as Aurelio Lampredi has recalled:

"One day Ferrari walked into the office and said, 'I have decided to divide this project office in two. From now on, Lampredi will occupy himself with projections and experiments in racing, and Colombo will occupy himself with mass production models'. So Colombo disappeared and eventually ended up back at Alfa-Romeo, where they still believed in superchargers. I rolled up my sleeves and set to work all on my own.

"As the 1500 supercharged Ferrari simply was not performing, Ferrari decided, 'Enough of superchargers! I've seen that they do not work. Let's make an aspirated engine instead' So I designed the V-12, 3.3 liter aspirated engine - 3.3. liters, because in my opinion, starting off small, we could then build up from there with more and more powerful engines."

The Swiss Grand Prix along the short straights and very fast, alarming curves of the Bremgarten circuit, saw a grinning Dr. Nino Farina, victorious in the Alfa 158, with both Ascari and Villoresi retiring with engine trouble.

Then, at the Belgian Grand Prix at Spa-Francorchamps, Alberto turned up with the first unsupercharged 3.3. liter, aspirated Ferrari. Although it turned out a 1-2-4 Alfa-Romeo benefit for Fangio, Fagioli and Farina - Alberto's tenacious and superbly regular driving took him into 5th place; he might even have done better if his tyre treads had not come away twice.

Thus, by mid-1950, the Points Score in the World Championship contest saw Farina with 22 points, Fagioli 18, Fangio 17, Rosier 10 and Ascari 8.

By this time, Dr. Farina, 45 years-old, had made it known privately and publicly that it was *he* who wanted to be the 1st World Champion, no matter what the costs. Known not only for his strict adherence to physical fitness (gymnastics, correct diet, teetotal, mountain air, sunshine etc.), but also for his irritability, Nino Farina was determined that Alfa-Romeo should honor him as a loyal Italian, rather than favor an Argentinian. Why, in his opinion, should General Peron, President of the Argentine Republic, be able to "make sure" that friend Fangio be equipped with the fastest car in the world, no matter what the cost? "But excuse me - I, Farina, have raced for Alfa-Romeo for years! Why does this gentleman who has arrived at the last minute, have to have the car that I should get?" Through the 1950 Season, this cold-blooded master of motor-racing technique, placing ruthlessness before chivalry, literally lived on his nerves and drove like a madman -protected only by his patron saint, the Holy Madonna della Conciliata of Turin! Ironically, during that Season, Fangio learnt much about driving from his team-mate - and whenever he went off in one of his huffy moods, the Argentinian merely laughed it off.

The next technical move by Aurelio Lampredi, came at the end of July at the Grand Prix des Nations in Geneva. Alberto turned up with a O.8 liters more power under the bonnet of the aspirated Formula One car, Lampredi's 4.1 engine - and succeeded in maintaining a 2nd place behind Fangio, in front of the other "Alfisti" - before having to retire with a broken piston. Gigi, who was not so fortunate in this race, has recalled: "Before the race, we were there at the garage where they were working on our cars. In front of the garage was a cafe. At a certain point, there was a terrible storm, and we took shelter underneath the awning of the cafe. We had sat down and were about to order a drink, when Alberto suddenly shouted 'Cretino! Get up!' - 'Huh - what's up?' I replied, jumping out of my seat only to find that underneath there was this black kitten. I, a great lover of animals, naturally took the black kitten in my arms and stroked it, to Alberto's horror! Soon after, in the race, I was involved in an extremely serious accident. Alberto, of course, blamed the kitten."

Only seven laps from the Finish of the 69-lap race, Gigi, driving his 3.3. liter Ferrari at over 100 m.p.h., hit a patch of oil left by Alberto's car, skidded out of control, crashed through the light wooden barrier and plunged into an area packed with spectators, killing three of them and injuring twenty. Gigi was thrown out of the car onto the road, the Ferrari was irreparably damaged and Farina swerved to avoid the wreck and hit the straw bales. . . Gigi was 41 at the time and badly injured: fractured femur, cracked clavicle, face and head injuries.

Alberto's bad luck in Formula One was happily not echoed in Formula Two contests and on August 20, he competed in the 13th German Grand Prix, held after a lapse of ten years on the re-surfaced, famous 14.1 mile mountain circuit of the Nürburgring in the Eifel mountains between the Belgian

Frontier and the Valley of the Rhine.

Absent were the three 'Fs' - Fangio had entered a Maserati, so also his Argentinian team-mate Froilan Gonzalez, but scratched at the last moment. Absent also was Gigi, still recovering and in his place, Ferrari's chief test driver, Dorino Serafini - so that Alberto was up against various less marques such as the Jicey, the Veritas, AFM, HWM and Simca.

Watched by 400,000 spectators, Alberto took the red 2-liter Formula Two Ferrari sixteen times round those 172 corners, ever increasing his lead, while Serafini had retired on Lap 2 with gear trouble. At 10 laps, he led by $2\frac{1}{2}$ minutes. He had clearly planned to go through non-stop, although whether his tyres could hold out was a debatable point.

Then, towards the end of the race, at the Karussel, Alberto's Ferrari traversed the lip of that famous banked turn, the shock breaking half the spokes in his offside rear wheel. Sensing that something had happened at the rear of his car, Alberto nursed her very tenderly for the last few miles of the race. Crossing the line he returned to his pit, and his mechanics discovered, half with relief and half with excitement that the wheel could be rocked sideways on its hub and if Alberto had had to compete a further lap, it would probably have collapsed, denying him victory! Breathing a quiet sigh of relief, he learned that he had completed the 227 miles at an average 77.67 m.p.h., and was cheered as new *Ringmeister* of the German Circuit. Nor would this be the last time he would see victory in the Eifel mountains.

Three weeks later, Maranello sent two new Ferraris to Monza for the 21st Italian Grand Prix - these cars now powered by 4.5. liters, developing 330 h.p. at 6,500 r.p.m., were to be driven by Ascari and Serafini. Against these, Portello sent two new, more powerful Alfa-Romeos - Type 159s - to be driven by Farina and Fangio - backed up by a pair of 158s driven by Fagioli and Taruffi.

When in practice, Fangio clocked a fastest lap at 1' 58" 3 and Ascari *his* fastest 1' 58" 4 - the Alfa Romeo team realized with some concern that here was a car, virtually untried, that could at last match theirs.

On the morning of the race, Dr. Giuseppe Farina and his wife Else, went to church to attend a special mass - a last minute attempt to leave nothing to chance. He just *had* to win this race from Fangio if he were to clinch that World Title.

70,000 spectators turned up up on a sultry, overcast, threatening September 3 and before long the shouts of "Viva Fangio!" against "Viva Nino!" against "Ciccio! Ciccio!" had all been drowned by the vibrating crescendo of massed cars as they surged off the grid in a solid phalanx of shining metal and spinning wheels. The brilliant Aurelio Lampredi, emotionally so overcome by the public birth of his 4.5 liter "brainchild", aware of all the things that might go wrong, fainted to the ground in the Ferrari pit! Farina, Fangio and Sanesi in the Alfas, surged on ahead. After a slow start on Lap 14, Alberto charged past Farina to show willing and tried to egg him on to the point where he either lost his temper or blew up his engine, whereupon the Doctor re-passed two laps later. Ascari had hounded him from behind for a further 6 laps, when he slowed down and came to a halt - trouble with his axle. Abandoning his car on the circuit, Alberto walked back to the pits amidst universal commiserations from his fellow citizens.

But then on Lap 48, Serafini handed *his* 4.5. liter Ferrari over to Alberto, who went off in pursuit of the Doctor, who was now almost two minutes in the lead. The crowd now start to cheer as wildly as before. With gradually improving lap times, "Ciccio" lessened that gap by 30 seconds, coming in 2nd behind an elated Nino Farina, who had at last realized his ambition of becoming World Champion and was crowned accordingly. Final Score: Farina 30 points, against Fangio's 27, Fagioli's 24 and Ascari's 14.

Just under two months later, on October 15 1950, the Xth Penya Rhin Grand Prix and VIIth Copa Barcelona was held on the 3.9 miles Pedrables circuit, comprising one 1.72 mile straight and five corners on the outskirts of that Spanish town. It was a hot and dusty day.

Although the Alfa-Romeos were absent, the three 4 liter Ferraris made their presence known - arriving 1-2-3 in the hands of Ascari, Serafini and Taruffi in a 4.1 liter version. On the flying Kilometer of that circuit, Alberto, clothcapped, was clocked at 169,36 m.p.h., not to mention his fastest lap at 97.7 m.p.h. At last, Enzo Ferrari and Aurelio Lampredi could feel that they had something to challenge with, in the 1951 Season.

As for Alberto Ascari's personal record? Out of 28 races competed in, he had won eleven victories, which enable him to retain his Championship of Italy, 8 points ahead of Franco Cortese and 20 in front of Tadini and Fagioli. But for the son of Antonio Ascari, this simply was not good enough. Nothing less than the World Championship would do.

"A Tactical Error"

By the beginning of 1951, Gigi Villoresi was sufficiently recovered from his Geneva crash to decide to return to racing. But from now on, the inseparable pair would no longer be wearing cloth-caps, but hardened crash helmets. Gigi's was white, whilst Alberto's was light blue, contrasting nicely with the Ferrari flame-red with its yellow and black crest.

During the next five years, a pair of canvas trousers with front pockets, a "tummy" sticking out from under a short-sleeved, open-necked, light blue woollen vest, and an azure blue motorcyclist's "pudding basin" helmet would come to be the distinguishing features of "Ciccio" Ascari in the motor-racing pits of Europe, South America, Mexico and the U.S.A. More than that, his helmet became his lucky talisman and without it he would not race. Once, at Monza, someone stole his helmet. Alberto put notices in the major newspapers of the Italian Press, to the effect that if whoever had stolen his helmet did not return it within the week, he, Alberto Ascari, would never race again. The helmet was returned the next day. Why Blue? It seems that he just loved blue - blue bedspreads and sheets, blue wallpaper, blue curtains, blue shirts, blue soap - blue private cars (be they Jaguar, Mercedes, Lancia, Fiat or Ferrari). But then Gigi Villoresi also had blue private cars, and explains:

"We had two boxes, where we kept our helmets, goggles, gloves etc they were both painted azure blue. NOBODY - not even Mietta - was allowed to touch Alberto's box, except himself. One day he was out lapping in the Ferrari, and I had need of a little piece of white cotton wool to put in my ears, because in those days we did not have noise-padded helmets, and I had forgotten to bring my own. So I opened his box. On top were a pair of gloves, which I moved ever so carefully. Then I took a little piece of cotton wool. Then I put everything back *exactly* as I had found it. He stopped at the pits, opened his box and said, 'Hey! Who's been mucking about with my things!'

Obviously, I had put those gloves back, 2 millimeters out of place, no more."

Their first re-appearance together was in a Lancia Aurelia Sportscar, in late February, when they won the Sestriere Rally with 584,70 points. One fortnight later, they took two of the 4.5. liter Ferraris to Syracuse, where, after leading for 70 of the 80 laps, even making one of them the fastest at 95.6 m.p.h., Alberto was forced to retire with overheating, giving the much needed confidence gained from a new victory, to Gigi.

Two weeks later, they were beneath the French Pyrénées, competing in the Pau Grand Prix - where the pattern was repeated: following a fastest lap, Alberto retired on lap 47 and Gigi completed the remaining 63 laps in the lead.

Two weeks on and they found themselves behind the wheels of the Formula 2 Ferraris at the Marseilles Grand Prix.

Aurelio Lampredi remembers that: "At Marseilles, there was a big name who later died of old age, a Frenchman, who had a Ferrari exactly the same as ours, but who had not succeeded in making good lap times. In front of everyone, seeing he was French, he spoke badly about our car. 'It's no good, it doesn't go! It's here, there, up, down.' Therefore, we made a rare decision in the history of motorsport and I asked Alberto, 'Do me a favor, would you mind testing this French gentleman's car? They are ruining our name, in front of the whole of Marseilles, in front of France.' Alberto took that car and broke the track record!"

Alberto, on the other hand, had different memories of Marseilles: "I went out of my hotel to fetch the car and make some practice laps. A black cat slid between my legs. I tempted Fate all the same and went out onto the track. After four circuits, the brakes stuck suddenly and I was thrown out of the car. I returned to the hotel, but the following morning, this devil cat, bounding in front of me, took refuge under my car. I shivered. I decided not to climb on board, but asked a friend to take my car down onto the track for me. My friend agreed, but was it through my lack of experience or again because of the cat? During the race, whilst I was passing a slower Frenchman, he unexpectedly and without reason went outwards. To avoid hitting him, I had to veer off, my car slamming up against the external protection of the circuit, irreparably damaging my steering wheel."

Thus Gigi Villoresi scored his third, 1951 victory.

That Winter, Messrs, Ferrari and Lampredi had further developed the unsupercharged 4.5. liter Formula One car to where there were two sparking plugs for each of the 12 cylinders double ignition. Following encouraging tests of the "twin-plug" car at Modena Autodrome, Alberto was given one of them for the Ospedaletti Circuit of the San Remo Grand Prix on April 22.

The race - anti-clockwise round the 2.1 mile twisting circuit, was, without a withdrawn Alfa team, a Ferrari benefit. For the first 50 laps, Alberto and Gigi played the passing and re-passing game for 1st and 2nd places, whilst Serafini followed up in 3rd place. Then Alberto increased his lead to 12 seconds and Gigi collided with an abandoned Maserati, retiring with a smashed-in grill and leaking radiator. Alberto cross the line, a minute ahead of Serafini.

This victory was followed by a most unpleasant incident, reminiscent of Gigi's Geneva crash. Alberto entered a Ferrari 3000 sportscar in the Mille Miglia, that gruelling and frightening challenge, where on either side of the road, crowds two to three deep lean forwards to catch a better glimpse of competitors. Soon after the Start, he had arrived at the cross-roads between Lonato and Desenzano, when his car skidded on an oil patch. It left the road and crashed into the crowd. Several people were injured and Doctor Umberto Feliciani, the municipal doctor of Montichiari, died from his injuries. Alberto's only explanation was that he had been suddenly dazzled by the lights of a car coming out of a side street. Terribly shaken, he did what he could to help the injured and bereaved and decided to abstain from competing in that race in future years. . .

He was however back on the track on May 13 in the Formula Two Autodrome Grand Prix at Monza. Heat One: Ascari beats Villoresi; Heat Two: Villoresi beats Ascari. The Final: Ascari beats Villoresi and averages 101.77 m.p.h.

13 for Alberto may well have been an unlucky number, but as Lampredi has explained: "If a race began on the 13th or the

17th or a Friday, Alberto would play at "Scaramanzia", arguing 'This race may be on the 13th, but I began my practice runs on the 11th, therefore the 11th is the significant day."

One weekend later, "Ciccio" was not so lucky. On Lap 37 of the Colombiano Grand Prix at Genoa - the back of Alberto's Formula 2 Ferrari caught fire. With typical calm, Alberto put on the brake and was about to jump, when he found his foot caught in the steering wheel. While the flames licked him, Ascari, assisted by Biondetti and Franco degli Uberti, succeeded in freeing himself, but not without a severe burn to his right fore-arm. Gigi won his fourth race - against Alberto's two.

But in reality, all these races had merely been a limbering-up process, in preparation for the first World Championship confrontation between Portello and Maranello, Alfa-Romeo versus Ferrari - at the Swiss Grand Prix at Berne. May 27 was a very rainy and slippery day that witnessed, on a watery Bremgarten Grid, the Ferraris of Ascari, Villoresi and Taruffi up against a quartet of Alfa 159's, driven by Fangio, Farina, Sanesi and de Graffenried.

Fangio succeeded in making a fierce start that put him out in front of anyone else's "wash" (a fan of spray) - and kept his lead to the end of the 195 - mile race. Farina was next, pursued by Villoresi until Lap 13, when Gigi, so blinded by the spray, spun off the road, fortunately without damage to anyone. Alberto, still suffering badly from his burnt arm, simply was not on form. So the Ferrari attack was reduced to Piero Taruffi, who by superb driving through showerbaths of Swiss rain and spray succeeded in overtaking Dr. Farina, but was unable to take Fangio as well, the latter gaining 9 championship points.

Again, at the Belgian Grand Prix at Spa-Francorchamps, three red 1½ liter supercharged Alfa 159's and three red unsupercharged 4.5. liter "twin-plug" Ferraris sorted themselves out in a furious race, with top speeds of 160 m.p.h. -so that Dr. Farina, magnificently on form, averaging 114.32 m.p.h., won from Alberto, three minutes behind him, averaging 112.32 m.p.h., a decisive victory for the Four-Leaved Clover over the Rampant Horse. Fangio who had set a new lap record of 120.51 m.p.h., would have been placed second, but suffered an infuriating 14-minute pit stop, when mechanics were unable to remove a rear wheel and had to change the tyre itself on the rim, placing the Argentinian 4th.

At the end of these first two heats (Swiss and Belgian), the World Championship positions were: Farina 12; Fangio 10; Ascari and Taruffi 6, Villoresi 4.

In the weekend interrupting the fortnight before the next "grande epreuve", Alberto, just to show himself that his driving ability was not at fault, decided to go to Naples to contest the Grand Prix on the Posillippo Circuit. Gigi recalls: "At Naples, I went to collect him from the station at 5 o'clock in the morning. To get to the city center, where our hotel was situated, there was this long, wide avenue. Alberto was driving when suddenly he slammed on the brakes! A black cat was crossing that avenue. We now made a detour such as I have never known, through obscure side-streets and back alleys just so as to arrive at our hotel from a different route. When we did arrive, I had fallen asleep!"

Despite this, Alberto notched up an easy victory, one lap ahead of Schell in 2nd place; Gigi gave no competition, out of the race with gear lever trouble.

The European Grand Prix at Rheims saw the next major contest between the fish-mouthed Ferraris and the grinning Alfa-Romeos - three works against four works. And now, as part of the Ferrari team, in Taruffi's absence, appeared Froilan Gonzalez, Fangio's massive Argentinian compatriot but rival, a "Pampas Bull" hot with successes in the Argentine, a "cabezon" (Spanish for "stubborn, determined") who came to be loved by everyone.

In oppressively hot French weather, watched by 70,000 spectators, Ascari tangled fiercely with Fangio, frequently alternating for 1st place, hotly pursued by Farina and Villoresi. Then Alberto retired with gear trouble on Lap 10, Fangio took up a short-lived lead and then himself retired with magneto trouble. Fagioli (Alfa) and Gonzalez (Ferrari) now duelled their way past a flagging Villoresi. Soon after, for the honor among sportsmen, Fangio climbed into Fagioli's car and Ascari climbed into Gonzalez's car - and battle recommenced betwen the two top works drivers.

In Gigi's opinion: "In those days Fangio was certainly *not* superior to Alberto. Alberto's style was one of force and vehemence, very clean, where he took up a position on a curve. Fangio, often extremely lucky, initiated the style of dérapage, side slipping."

While Villoresi's Ferrari became increasingly sick, showering Gigi with oil and Nino Farina's Alfa suffered magneto trouble as well, the engines and skills of Fangio and Ascari seemed equally pitted against each other until the Ferrari developed brake trouble. "El Chueco" led "Ciccio" over the line by 58 seconds, with Villoresi 3rd in a Ferrari and Parnell 4th in his own, private "Thin Wall Special" Ferrari and Farina 5th.

From this hard-fought race, the points table for the World Championship now read: Fangio 15; Farina 14; Ascari 9.

But as Alfa-Romeo Engineer Satta, who had done his utmost to make the best of an old design with two-stage supercharging and special fuels - well knew, Aurelio Lampredi's new, unsupercharged Ferrari design was about to blossom as a force to be reckoned with. It was only a question of time before victory would prove it.

That day in question, July 13, 1951, was to be neither Alberto Ascari's nor Gigi Villoresi's. Rather, it was that of José Froilan Gonzalez in his year-old, single-plug Ferrari at the British Grand Prix at Silverstone. Ascari retired on lap 56 with gearbox trouble. Farina retired on lap 76 with clutch afire. Gonzalez, the ferocious "puma" duelled with the precise Fangio, his fellow Argentinian, on that short, twisty Northamptonshire circuit - so that it became an Argentinian benefit, with Villoresi, the Silverstone favorite in 3rd place. Enzo Ferrari cried tears of happiness and pride that day. For Alfa-Romeo's five-and-a-half years of domination had at last been broken. And also, in the opinion of Aurelio Lampredi, something else had changed that day. "My friend and brother, Alberto Ascari had arrived willingly at Maranello, but from the outset it seemed as if, at the back of his mind, there lingered doubts about our Ferrari car. 'Yes it is a beautiful car, however the Alfa . . . But when 'Pepé' Gonzalez scored that first true victory in the 4.5. at Silverstone, for Alberto the myth of Alfa was at once dispelled, and he was 110% with us."

Keen to contribute to the conquest of Alfa-Romeo, Alberto's eyes now turned towards Germany and the Nürburgring where the XIth German Grand Prix was to be held. If he were to increase his points score to anywhere near Fangio's, he would certainly have to work hard on a victory there - the Grosser Preis having just been made into a qualifying round for that so keenly desired World Championship.

89 bends to the left, 85 to the right, cornering *ad nauseam* on the 14-mile circuit, twisting and plunging erratically through the Eifel Mountains, past Castle Nürburg and the endless pine forests - climbing uphill to empty skylines, trying to remember what action to take over the next brow - a 3 Kilometer straight, spanning two hump-backed bridges that made the car jump into the air and slam down again.....this was the Ring.

Alberto was still holding his Ferrari straight, deliberately holding his foot off the brake pedal so as not to damage the delicate Elektron brake drum, therefore travelling at 60 m.p.h. minus that *wheel;* when Hawthorn, Fangio and Farina slammed past with a concentrated roar of exhaust. After some 200 meters, the crippled Ferrari overshot its pit with Alberto gesticulating wildly, only coming to a halt beyond the end of the pit road. With the engine still running, Alberto just sat there waiting, while a mechanic rushed out with a wheel-jack, thrusting it under the front end.

Thus supported, this master of cool, went into reverse, and the mechanic steered the car backwards to its pit. With Alberto just sitting in that cockpit, absolutely calm, it took them 4 minutes 12 seconds to check the brake drum, find a new hubcap, borrowed from the pit of Maserati entry Enrico Platé, and fit another wheel. After which, Alberto re-joined the fray amidst thunderous cheering. His next flying Lap was a Formula 2 record.

Lampredi: "In those days a driver had to be sensitive to the fact that a car had a soul that needed both discipline and nursing if it were to remain loyal and sincere. Otherwise it would warn its driver, 'Look out, because you have just made

THE MAN WITH TWO SHADOWS

another mistake. If you do it next time, I will throw you out! At which the driver must have the courage and intelligence to say, 'Yes, you may try to throw me out, but I'll keep and hold on you just the same!'"

But by this time, Mike Hawthorn was leading until the close of Lap 7 when his team senior, by twenty-three years, Dr. Farina, stormed past into first place. For the Doctor had not forgotten his defeat on this track the previous year. Tiring and perhaps dispirited, Hawthorn was then caught by Fangio.

By dint of fine driving, Alberto had pulled himself back into 5th place by Lap 9, when he came back into the pits with smoke coming from the drum. Following a brief discussion, Ugolini, the pit manager, flagged Gigi into the pits, who readily swapped cars with his ex-pupil.

Gigi recalls: "Many times, when I handed over my car to Alberto, it was in the interests of the reputation of the company for whom we were racing - Maserati, Ferrari, etc. - so that they could say 'Ferrari won this race.'"

The quartet of Alfa 159s resumed their battle against the quartet of 4.5 liter Ferraris, very much less confident. The Alfa's had to refuel twice, the Ferraris only once. Watched by 180,000 spectators, Fangio immediately overtook Farina, and led a follow-my-leader of Farina, Gonzalez and Ascari. Having overhauled the two others, Alberto - racing number 71 - took Fangio on lap 4 and they pressed on, nose to tail, Alberto widening the gap by 2.2. seconds, using his familiarity with the track, gained the previous year, to full advantage.

After a pit stop, Fangio now returned to the race after 38 seconds, now in 3rd place. On lap 8, an infuriated Dr. Farina pulled back into the Alfa pits, flung off his helmet and retired with gearbox trouble. lap 9: race leader, Ascari stopped to take on 180 liters of fuel and rear tyres in 50 seconds, while Gonzalez and Fangio moved ahead. Then after a fast lap, Gonzalez made *his* pit stop, whereupon Ascari overtook Fangio again and led on. Then Fangio retaliated with two lap speed records, one after the other, overtaking and spacing himself ahead of Alberto by 14.5 seconds. While Pietsch crashed in his Alfa and Bonetto retired with *his,* Fangio was left with the sole surviving Alfa and up against a phalanx of five

Ferraris. With only 14 seconds' lead, he made a flurried pit stop which cost him 44 seconds when his Alfa stalled after new tyres and a refuel. At lap 15, Ascari led by 56.4 seconds and was still pulling away, with consummate mastery of the German track.

Amazingly, with three laps remaining and over a minute's lead, Alberto came past the pits, gesticulating at Ferrari's new Race Manager, Nello Ugolini (ex-Maserati) and pointing at his rear tyres. Next time round, as Lampredi recalls: "Ascari arrives at the pits and stops. 'Change my tyres' he says. 'What do you mean? Those tyres are alright for the rest of the race. Get back onto the - ' 'Change my tyres! Change those tyres now or I'm going to climb down from this car.' 'Alright! God! Get to it, boys! Change the damned tyres!' The mechanics weren't ready for it. The Ferrari was swiftly jacked up; then a wheelnut stuck; 20,25, 30 seconds went by. The Ferrari team was frantic. Alberto remained calm. He was away after 39 seconds with still no sign of Fangio. Then Juan Manuel came with only top gear left - but came too late. Alberto, benefitting from those new tyres, beat his great Argentinian rival and friend over the Line by 30.5 seconds. 3rd place went to Gonzalez (Ferrari); 4th place to Villoresi (Ferrari); 5th place to Taruffi (Ferrari); 6th place to Fischer (Ferrari) - an overwhelming Ferrari victory.

After the race, Lampredi asked him "In Heaven's name why did you take that risk?"

"I came in because otherwise people would have said that I won because I made only *one* pit stop - instead *I also* made two stops - and one of them a SURPRISE!"

But Alberto also knew, as did others, that although Dr. Farina could no longer endanger Fangio's grasp of the World Championship, he, Alberto Ascari, was catching up.

Now followed two lesser Grand Prix races on Italian soil. On August 15 for the Pescara Circuit alongside the Adriatic, which Alfa-Romeo did not turn up for, three 4.5. liter Ferraris turned up.

When on lap 1, Alberto broke down on the course with loss of oil, he decided to walk back to the pits to "borrow" Gigi's Ferrari for the remainder of the race. At this stage, Gigi had been winning, but had also turned up at the pits with his rear wheels down to their canvas. His car had been jacked up, and

THE MAN WITH TWO SHADOWS

the rear wheels were being changed, when Alberto keen to be off in pursuit of Gonzalez, clambered into the cockpit. He tried to drive away with the jack still in place! When he did eventually return to the track - the failure of the Ferrari's rear axle again put him out of a race won by Gonzalez.

Aurelio Lampredi recalls: "Racing in this country and then that country, we became rather like a travelling circus - you had the clowns, who were mechanics, and the acrobats and bare-back horse-riders who were the drivers. In those days the troupe, be they drivers, mechanics or engineers, ate and chatted as friends. If there was aggression, it was while the race was on."

Two weeks passed, and the Grand Prix "circus" found itself 170 miles further south along the Adriatic Coast for the Bari Grand Prix - where Fangio with Farina, and Ascari with Villoresi and Gonzalez came out of their respective corners for a further punch-up. After another furious Alfa-Ferrari duel, Farina retired with a broken piston on lap 7; Alberto's car back-fired and caught fire on lap 19, fortunately without injury to the driver, then on lap 31 a shunt caused Villoresi's car to lose its oil pressure. For the remainder of the race, Fangio gradually increased his lead from compatriot Gonzalez, whose Ferrari had gearbox trouble until "El Chueco" had won by a full minute. This win, with three Ferraris *hors de combat,* persuaded Portello that they might again tussle with more success with Maranello at the Italian Grand Prix at Monza.

To this end, they now brought out their final ace - the revised and re-designated Alfa-Romeo 159M, M, standing for "Maggiorata" or "increased" to 450 h.p. as against Ferrari's 400, In fact, they produced four 159Ms - and during practice that September, Fangio did a phenomenal lap at 124.53 m.p.h. smashing all previous records and startling the Ferrari team considerably. But then Ferraris had also been revised with increase fuel capacity in longer tails.

September 16 was a hot, gloriously sunny day and saw the Autodrome crammed full of thousands of spectators - spectators divided in their loyalties - to Alfa Romeo the Milanese Company or to Alberto Ascari the Milanese ace driver - one way or other, intensely patriotic.

Hardly any wind blew across the Lombardy Plain to move the lazy clouds of exhaust smoke that drifted up from a pack of flame-red cars - four Alfas and five Ferraris. As the flag fell, Fangio roared out into the lead, but by lap 3, Ascari had just a two cars length lead on Fangio. By lap 12 Fangio and Ascari in a superb, awe-inspiring combat were as if glued together. Then on lap 13, the tread of one of Fangio's tyres came off abruptly and as the Argentinian "limped" into his pit, that tyre exploded with a bang. He was away in 34 seconds, but by that time Alberto was firmly in the lead and was never caught again. On lap 34, he made a pit stop to refuel and have his tyres changed. Aurelio Lampredi was in the pits: "They were speed-filling his fuel tank using air pressure. But the pressure was too high, so that the flexible length of tube separated itself from the large piece of steelpipe, 120mm in diameter, complete with valve, which went down into the tank. While the steel tubing remained sticking out of the tank, the flexible tube began to flay around in the air, spraying fuel all over us, including some officials and a couple of carabinieri! Then it whacked a mechanic in the stomach, knocking him to the ground.

"Alberto, seeing all this, rather than wait precious seconds until the chaos cleared, drove off, with the fuel tank lid still open and the steel pipe sticking out. While we busied ourselves cleaning the wretched fuel off our clothes and faces, amazingly, Alberto had driven round Monza - Monza no less! - at 100 m.p.h., steering with only one arm, while he had stretched the other one behind and pulled out the offending piece of tubing!"

On lap 56, he came in again for a further wheel-change and refuel that took 40 seconds, then pressed on with an impregnable lead to complete the 312-mile course at an average 115.49 m.p.h., having slowed up for the last ten laps with a somewhat fatigued V-12 engine. Gonzalez came in 2nd, forty-five seconds later, followed by Farina in the sole surviving Alfa and Villoresi a further half lap behind. Fangio had retired half-way with piston failure.

Lampredi: "At the end of a race where nearly all his Alfa's had retired one by one, until the sole survivor had limped over the Finish Line in neutral, Engineer Gallo of Alfa-Romeo wanted to meet the designer of this reliable Ferrari. So I was

THE MAN WITH TWO SHADOWS

taken over by Sanesi and Guidotti to the Alfa-Romeo pit. The first thing Gallo said, was - 'But you can't be Lampredi? You're so young'. To which, I replied, 'Sir, was it my fault that I was born so late?' Then Gallo smiled and said, 'Today, you, young sir, have indeed killed the supercharged racing car.'

Not long after the race, Alberto presented Aurelio with a photograph in memory of the 1951 Monza victory. Written at the foot of it are the words: "Io sono Ascari in quanto tu sei Lampredi. Ma tu sei Lampredi in quanto io sono Ascari" ("I am Ascari in as much as you are Lampredi. But you are Lampredi in as much as I am Ascari").

Alberto Ascari may have been an exhausted victor that evening, but his heart and mind thrilled to the exciting and now real possibility of a World Title which might be clinched at the final race in Barcelona. For Fangio had 28 points from five races, and Ascari 25 from four events. Fangio's score was made up of 9,5,6,1 and 7. Ascari's total from 6,3,8,8. Thus Juan Manuel could total 37 points for a win and the fastest lap, and Alberto 34. If Fangio took 2nd place, he would have 33 points for his best five performances, which would be equalled if Ascari were to win, and bettered were he also to make the fastest lap.

Thus, the showdown for the 1951 Championship would be sweated out over 70 laps of the Spanish Grand Prix at Barcelona, on Sunday October 28.

Pedralbes Circuit measured 3.93 miles, part of which was the distinctly bumpy, but wide, Avenida del Generalissimo Franco - long and broad, at the end of which road there was a sharp, uphill climb to a first right-hander and thereafter the circuit was completed by wiggling back through the streets on the residential outskirts of the city at the foot of the Pedralbes hills.

Alberto arrived there, fresh from a Formula 2 victory the weekend before at Modena, and went into his practice laps with determined enthusiasm, alongside three other 24-plug versions of the 4.5. liter Ferrari, driven by Villoresi, Gonzalez and Taruffi. He completed one lap at 2'10" 59 - 108,1 m.p.h. shattering all previous records - and two minutes faster than Fangio's best.

In hot, sunny weather, some 250 - 300,000 people witnessed

nineteen ear-rending cars complete their first laps - Ascari-cum-Fangio going round like magnet to metal. Trouble started when on lap 6 Ferrari-driver Taruffi came into the pits with a tread flapping on a rear tyre - strange, because Piero Taruffi was always easy on his tyres. Then Villoresi came in with his nearside tyre literally in ribbons. Then Ascari went past, pointing at his rear tyres and came in on lap 9 with practically nothing showing on both wheels but the casing - losing 32 seconds on the wheel-change. It soon became obvious that the bumpy and abrasive surface of the circuit was playing havoc with the Ferrari tyres. If they had chosen the wrong size tyres 16" instead of 18" as Alfa were using), then that was a fatal, tactical error. But, in Aurelio Lampredi's recollection, it was something far more deadly: "Blowing up the tyres on a hoop leaning against a wall, was without our knowing it, pulling off those tyre treads. When we realized this, it was too late!"

Fangio in the Alfa 159M, maintained and increased his lead, hitting speeds of 180 m.p.h. on the General Franco Straight spacing himself almost a minute ahead of whoever could take 2nd place - be it Gonzalez, Farina or Taruffi. Alberto's attempt to climb back up was heroic, but he was again forced in with tyre-shredding on lap 17 (losing 29 seconds) and yet again on lap 27 (losing 34 seconds). His final ignominy came on lap 55 when Fangio actually lapped him. He came in at the end of that race, having pulled himself up from 14th to 4th place, completely exhausted, soaked in oil and sweat, and almost overcome by fumes from the engine. Gigi had retired on lap 48 with engine trouble.

Fangio had just notched up 31 points to his 25. Alberto had failed to get a World Championship for the second year running - not through lack of driving skill, nor through an unreliable engine or transmission - but through tyres that were 1 inch too thin! Yet like the sportsman he was, Alberto Ascari congratulated the victorious and elated Juan Manuel Fangio and arranged to send him a silver plate, suitably inscribed. For Fangio, hosted as the idol of General Franco's Spain, then as the idol of General Peron's Argentina - the victory cele-brations were gloriously sweet. Farina again protested that if Alfa-Romeo had not favored Fangio, he might well have retained his World Championship.

Undaunted by his ill-fortune and refreshed by a holiday, Alberto and Gigi were off again two weeks later, this time across the Atlantic Ocean to drive a Ferrari 2500 sportscar in the Carrera Pan Americana. They competed against about one hundred other cars, mostly big American models, in an open road race from the South to the North of Mexico, taking five days of rallydriving. Gigi recalls: "Carrera Mexicana was a unique race infinitely more varied than the Mille Miglia because the first section involved mountainous hairpins, 2600 meters above sea level, making good carburation extremely difficult. Later on you had long, dusty 50 kilometer straights without a single bend and it became a question of speed.

"Exactly the same thing happened to us in Mexico as had happened in Barcelona. After the mountainous section, we arrived on the Plains with flat, bumping, treadless tyres and no more spaces. Taruffi and Chinetti in their Ferrari, lost fewer tyres because they had blown up their pressures a little higher."

Following Taruffi-Chinetti, Ascari and Villoresi came 2nd in this race having averaged 87.47 m.p.h. for 22 hours, proving to their Press critics that they were not just Grand Prix Circuit drivers but could also excel in long distance road racing.

Not long after the race, Alberto and Gigi enjoyed a spell of deep-sea fishing off Acapulco Bay, in the turquoise Pacific Ocean. "There we were in this motorboat, driven by this magnificent black with a resplendant gold chain hanging round his neck, at the end of which was suspended this magnificent gold medal, and accompanied by a nimble young teenage deckhand. Alberto and I were strapped into chairs holding these vast rods, when 50 meters away, two huge black marlin decided to dispossess us of our baits! The deck hand was tremendous; he gave each of our rods a jerk and we had them on our lines! The Marlin is one of the fastest fishes in the world and it took us over an hour to hoist those two superb examples each over two meters long, out of the water, pulling-in and paying-out all the time, the motor-boat even going into reverse so as not to break our lines. We arrived back at the Acapulco Fishing Club and had our photograph taken, standing next to our suspended catch - as Grand Prix Fishermen!"

At the end of that year, Alberto retained his Italian Championship title with 42 points, as against Gigi's 34, Dr. Farina's 27 and Taruffi's 23. In the Formula 2 Championship, however, Franco Cortese beat him by 4 points.

But Alberto's intense, hazel-brown eyes were still resolutely fixed on the World Championship title.

"An Italian At the Brickyard"

It was in 1952 that an ironic sequence of events paved the way to World supremacy for Alberto Ascari. In 1952, Alfa-Romeo withdrew from racing. They had been hoping to produce a lighter, more powerful car for the season, but a badly needed subsidy from the Italian Government was not forthcoming. Their works drivers dispersed: while Farina signed up with Ferrari as one of their works drivers alongside Alberto, Fangio decided to free-lance, signing up with both Maserati and with the developing BRM (British Racing Machine) concern: the 53 year-old Fagioli was soon to be fatally injured whilst practicing for the Monaco sportscar GP in his Lancia Aurelia.

With the Formula One V-16 BRM still mechanically immature, race organizers across Europe realized that any Formula One race would end up a dull, high-speed procession of V-12, 4.5. liter Ferraris. So to encourage International competition, they began to go over to 2-liter Formula Two races.

The IInd Syracusa Grand Prix on Sicily's South-East Coast on March 16 turned out a Formula Two Ferrari benefit, watched by 100,000 people. Villoresi's car caught fire just as the Starter's flag fell. Then Alberto took a bend too straight and crashed through straw bales and into a solid wall, 1 meter high, 4 meters of which crumbled under impact with the robust Ferrari. Unhurt but angry, Alberto raced on in pursuit of his team-mates. So regular was his driving that he computed a sequence of laps identical to the 10th of a second (2'14"3) - and after a high-speed duel, he came in 1st, averaging 88.4. m.p.h. for the 60 laps.

Three weeks later, the Turin Grand Prix was held on the Valentino Park Circuit, watched by 60,000 spectators. Two, specially-engined 4.5. liter Ferraris turned up, driven by Farina and Ascari - in preparation for their challenge at the Indianapolis "500" race in the U.S.A. the following month. There were also four further Ferraris on the Grid - and the music of six Ferraris is something to be heard in itself!

The start saw Alberto sweep into the lead, with Gigi hot in pursuit, whilst an infuriated Dr. Farina was held back on the Starting line with, of all things, a stuck gear lever. He finally went off in furious pursuit, determined not to be beaten by that young upstart rival, Ascari, and setting up the fastest lap at 77.47 m.p.h., all the time gaining seconds on that inseparable duo. But then on lap 33, Farina of Turin, while attempting to overtake Taruffi on the curve of the Palazzo delle Belle Arti - went off course, after spinning round twice, overturned twice and ended up in the escape field, fortunately without hitting the crowd. Farina, thrown out of the car, hit the asphalt, banging his head violently on the ground; fortunately he was wearing a crash helmet. He got up and, applauded by the crowd and embraced by his wife, limped back to the pits, in a state of nervous shock. He had broken three ribs and his Indianapolis Ferrari was a write-off.

Meantime, Alberto pressed on in the lead. But on lap 56, with only four laps to the end of the race - the Ferrari engine roar faltered - insufficient carburation? Yes, from a cracked fuel tank. He continued, despite the stink of petrol spillage on the track, until his car came to a halt on lap 57. Gigi Villoresi, typically modest, commented as victor, that he preferred more dazzling victories!

Perhaps the most significant aspect of the Formula One Turin Grand Prix was that, with BRM scratching their entry at the last moment, it became a race between drivers, not between marques or nationalities.

Therefore, the FIA (Féderation Internationale de l'Automobile) decided that the 1952 World Championship contest was to be run on the 2-liter unsupercharged/500 c.c. supercharged ruling - or in other words, Formula Two. This meant, ironically that the 4.5. liter Ferraris, so painstakingly and brilliantly developed by Aurelio Lampredi, had become almost redundant overnight - almost but not quite.

Following two superb Formula Two victories at Pau and

Marseilles, Alberto, a great lover of "Westerns", those movies involving cowboys, cavalry, Indians, rodeos, races, stampedes and gunfights - went to the United States of America, with a special 4.5. liter 420 horsepower Ferrari to race in the Indianapolis "500" in Indiana State.

In 1946, Gigi Villoresi had taken a pre-War 8-cylinder, double-supercharged Maserati to "The Brickyard", the nickname for Indianapolis Motor Speedway: "I had both Guerrino Bertocchi and a black mechanic helping me and although the car suffered from magneto trouble on the 10th and 40th laps - the plugs had to be changed each time and we lost 10 minutes. I came in 6th. But at that time, the Americans were also using pre-War cars. It was only afterwards that they began to construct cars specially designed for turning to the left."

Six years later, when Ferrari agreed to send the magnificent 4.5. liter car to Indianapolis, as Lampredi explains: "In Italy, the information we had about Indianapolis was very vague. We knew how many bricks there were on the track and how they had constructed the pagoda. But the necessary speed, the type of cars, how they were constructed - zero information. Yet as a sporting challenge, Indy was fascinating.

"Before going, we had put our 490 h.p. car through 500 Kilometers of trials at Monza and it had *never* stopped; so we thought we could win, with Alberto driving with his hands in his pockets. We were in for a surprise."

Behind him, he left cars that were not as powerful as his, arriving at "The Brickyard", to run against cars that were not only more powerful, but 100 Kg lighter in weight, and specially designed and developed to run for 500 - not 200 - miles around an utterly regular, left-handed, rectangular course, measuring 9.99 miles; four deceptively similiar, worrying curves to the left, two long straights and two short ones, just enough space to straighten up the car between one curve and another. It was hardly the Nürburgring or Bremgarten. Instead it was a hypnotically dull lesson in geometric driving for 200 laps.

From his arrival at the beginning of May - a month before the race, Alberto realized that not only must he adapt *his* driving technique, but that the 4.5. liter Ferrari would have to be improved in something of a hurry if it were even to qualify. Unable to quickly take it back home to Modena, he was fortunate in having with him, two superb Ferrari mechanics, Meazza and Reggiani to make the necessary modifications.

In learning about the track and understanding its almost remote-control requirements, Alberto was helped by old Tommy Milton, who had raced on the Monza Autodrome with Jimmy Murphy back in the early 1920's, in Antonio Ascari's day and also won the "500" twice himself (in 1921 and 1923.) In those early trials, Ascari progressively increased his speed from 95 up to 115 up to 120, then up to just below 130 m.p.h.

Thereafter, the Ferrari Special started having difficulties in getting any faster and it seemed as if a disappointed Ascari would have to give up the idea of qualifying.

"Telegrams flew backwards and forwards from Maranello to Indy," Lampredi remembers. "Eventually, as a last-minute measure we constructed and tested a special quadruple carburettor system at Maranello that would give him about 15 horsepower extra. Then myself, Nello Ugolini and Giovanni Canestrini went to Milan Airport with our carefully packed carburettors and took off for the States. Each time we stopped at various airports - such as Glasgow - to change 'planes, I made sure that the package containing those carburettors was still with us. When from New York we arrived at Indianapolis, our precious package was missing - Porca Miseria! - They had made a mistake and sent it on to St. Louis!"

When it was re-located and flown back to Indianapolis, mechanics worked night and day, Alberto re-testing the car, the gear ratios being slightly modified, before the Ferrari team decided to ask for a "free track" to attempt the qualifying laps.

On Saturday May 24, at 6 o'clock in the evening, just before the track closed, the Ferrari Special was wheeled out and its engine started up. By this time, the Americans had come to show a great deal of respect and friendship towards this determined Italian, who was always saying the only word he knew in English - "Fine, fine" - and had come out to beat them at their own game. And part of that game was to set up a qualifying speed over four laps that would place you among that fixed number of 33 cars and drivers allowed to start in the race; and in 1952, some 83 cars and drivers had been in the running.

Everyone watched him with great interest - and high anxiety where the Italian team was concerned - as he made one preliminary lap at sustained speed to make sure all was in order. Then, as he lifted his arm, passing in front of the timekeeper's box Alberto Ascari's trial began. Many stopwatches were depressed.

So far, that Ferrari Special had not shown better than 132 m.p.h. - but now, with clockwork regularity, it lapped at 107"5 - or in other words 135.5, 135.5, 135.5 and 135.5 - which was not 33rd fastest, but 25th fastest! The Italians went wild, the best of American motorsport's drivers and fans cheered and applauded for over a minute and Speedway President, Wilbur Shaw, who had great admiration for "Ciccio", personally congratulated him. Perhaps more stunning was the fact that there were only 14/100ths of a second difference between his fastest and slowest lap and that, no argument, was an Indianapolis record in itself! Lampredi: "It was a very moving, unforgettable experience!"

Now Enzo Ferrari had also supplied three 4.5. Ferraris to Americans, Howard Keck, Johnny Mauro and the Grand Piston Ring concern. The Grant car qualified, but 1950 "500" winner, Johnny Parsons, preferred to drive an American Offenhauser-powered car in the race. Johnny Mauro's fastest lap at 132 m.p.h. was too slow to qualify and Bill Vukovich was able to set a better qualifying speed of 138 m.p.h. in the Fuel Injection Special than he could in Keck's Ferrari.

Indeed, of the 33 cars that qualified, 29 of them were powered by 4-cylinder "Offy" or Offenhauser engines. But unlike the mass of red (Maseratis, Alfa-Romeos and Ferraris) that came to the Starting Grid of a European Grand Prix - the line-up for "Indy 500" was like a rainbow: cream, silver, yellow, blue, turquoise, gold, orange , black etc. - a multi-colored mass of Specials. Alberto in the red Ferrari (Racing Number 12) in Row 7, was flanked by Art Cross of Brunswick, M.J. in his cream, black and red Bowes Seal Fast Special and Jimmy Bryan of Phoenix, Arizona in his red and silver Pete Schmidt Special - all described as "Rookie" drivers.

It was May 30 and a Friday. In the days preceding the race, Alberto had been asked to fill in a questionnaire about himself. 33 years old, 5ft 8" high, 180 lbs. heavy; other favorite sports: skiing and canoeing; Profession: Car Dealer; Reason for Becoming a Racing Driver "per la passione sportiva dell Automobile" - "for the sporting passion of the car". He had even been given two whole lines to write down his superstitions - and had left them completely blank!

When, however, he later explained his bad luck that day in Indiana, Alberto Ascari, a truly superstitious Roman Catholic, blamed it on a Friday!

Lampredi recalls the tactics he and Alberto decided to adopt for the race: "To have him make a pit stop every 50 laps to refuel and change tyres. The Americans were taking almost 2 minutes to refuel, while we were taking 18 seconds - which meant that in four re-fuelling stops, we could seize four laps. Alberto was to do the first section at 6,500 revs, then 6,500 again, then into the final offensive."

Alberto later recalled: "In the race, I made the first laps at a reduced speed, wanting to study my opponents and the behavior of our engine. When I was persuaded I could throw myself forward, I accelerated from 21st up to 7th place. I now began to feel more at ease and to think that, if bad luck did not pursue me, I might be able to arrive 3rd, or perhaps even 2nd. I had already decided to wait for refuelling and to make my offensive, when on lap 40, disaster struck...."

He was holding his Ferrari to the smooth line of the raised North-West corner that would take him onto the next straight, while it bounced, jerking and skidding towards the impregnable concrete wall. At this moment, the outside rear wheel, in particular its hubcap, the one doing the most to resist centrifugal force, collapsed, crashing the lurching car onto the pavement in a shower of sparks. The Ferrari Special, Number 12, now made a big "pirola", describing a large arc, at first towards the dreaded wall and then looping down into the unpaved infield where it came to rest in a cascade of ploughed earth. The shutters of a hundred cameras blinked. Ascari was out of the race. The man who never lost his calm climbed out of the car and helped assistants to push it to a less dangerous area.

Lampredi: "He returned to the pits. He did not say a word for the rest of the race. Both our heads hung low that day, because we had had an easy victory in sight, and we had lost our chance."

The race continued - a duel between Bill Vukovich "The Mad Russian" (of Yugoslav parentage) in the Fuel Injection Special, up against 22 year-old big blonde Troy Ruttman, the transplanted Oklahoman, who had risen to fame in the California hot rod ranks before he was old enough to drive on the highways. After 400 miles out of the 500, just 22 cars were left. Vukovich looked like winning, but then just eight laps before the Finish, a steering pin broke and his car, Number 26, skidded into the North-East wall. Ruttman raced on in his Agajanian Couvrante Special to become the youngest winner in "500" history, averaging 128.922 m.p.h.

Slightly bruised, Alberto Ascari and the Ferrari team returned home to Milan and Modena, waxing enthusiastic about the American way of life and of automobile racing, and determined to win the "Indy 500", the following year. Sadly the politics of Enzo Ferrari was not to permit this. But the 34 year-old Italian who went to "The Brickyard" was always to treasure his AAA armband, on the back of which was written, "To Alberto Ascari - A Grand Guy".

It is perhaps significant that whilst he was away in America, the Paris Grand Prix was held at the fateful Montlhéry, road and track circuit, Ferrari sending three works cars driven by Farina, Villoresi and Taruffi. If Alberto had been at home, would he, one wonders, have competed at Montlhéry, and raced past "Ascari Corner", where the memorial to his father still stood? As it is, Farina ended up in a ditch that day, but without injury.

Alberto now prepared to enter back into European-style racing against his arch-rival, Juan Manuel Fangio, to compete for the 1952 World Title - albeit in Formula Two races. Their first encounter was to be the Autodrome Grand Prix at Monza. Fangio had spent *his* first three months, winning six races in South America in a Ferrari. He arrived at Monza having competed the day before in a BRM in Ireland for the Ulster Tourist Trophy and retired, then having driven overnight from

Paris to Monza. He started that race, exhausted and without any practice, driving a Maserati "Six" and crashing it disasterously on the Lesmo corner. He was thrown out of the car and broke a bone in his neck. Lucky to escape with his life, Fangio was unconscious for many days. Eventually he left Milan Hospital with his neck in plaster armor-plating to hold it still, returning to the Argentine to recover, *slowly*. The significance of this crash meant that Ascari's major rival was out of racing for the rest of 1952...

But, of course, there was still Doctor Farina of Turin, determined not to let a man from Milan, twelve years his junior, outstrip or cheat him of the honors that, he felt, should rightly be his. This was shown at the Autodrome Grand Prix, contested over two 35-lap heats. Alberto won the first heat. Then in the second, they were literally swapping aggressively for 1st place, one after the other, as serious rivals; then Alberto's badly lubricated camshaft seized up and while he was pushing the car back to the pits, the Doctor went into an impregnable lead that he kept to the 35th lap.

One fortnight later Farina and Ascari were up against each other on one of the most difficult circuits in Europe, along the precise, high-speed straights of the Belgian circuit - Spa-Francorchamps. Heavy rain had soon created a soaking wet, slippery course. But after a duel with Jean Behra in the Blue Gordini and with Farina in the Ferrari, Alberto pulled away, spacing himself first 24 seconds, then over a minute ahead of the Doctor. He won at over 103 m.p.h. - in a style that would have made Antonio Ascari, who had also scored a decisive victory at Spa some 27 years before, definitely proud of his son.

A French Championship had been inaugurated that year, comprising eight little, 3-hour Grand Prix: La Baule, Comminges, Marseilles, Pau, Montlhéry, Les Sables d'Olonne and Rouen - the last mentioned also ranking as the French Grand Prix.

On June 29, the Ferrari works drivers went to Rheims, the fourth event, to combat against three 2-liter Gordinis, driven for France by Manzon, Bira and Jean Behra, former French motorcycle champion gone to four wheels. For this race, the Rheims circuit had been made infinitely faster by the

A characteristically determined Antonio in the pits at
the 1924 Italian Grand Prix.

Young Alberto (in the leather hat) gazes admiringly at his victorious father, who shares his triumph with his boss Signor Romeo.

Montlhéry 1925. Antonio died later in the race.

An inexperienced Alberto being reprimanded by his
mentor Gigi Villoresi (French Grand Prix 1947).

'Ciccio' Ascari.

The implacable, almost disdainful, racing style.

The all-powerful quartet: (l - r) Alberto, Farina, Villoresi and Fangio.

Winning - the Ascari trademark.

The Ascari-Villoresi bond extended beyond the track, as did their need for competition.

Alberto gaining his elusive Mille Miglia victory in 1954
in a Lancia.

The line up for his last race at Monaco in July 1955.
His car bears the date of Antonio's and his own ultimate
demise.

The remains of Alberto's car after his fatal crash in training.

elimination of a right angle in the village of Gueux. Ascari, Villoresi and Farina had thought they would have little trouble in beating the French.

But from the Start, Jean Behra raced his Gordini into the lead, which despite Alberto's several attacks, he maintained in a style that exhilerated the partisan French crowd. At the end of lap 14, Alberto pulled into the pits with an engine overheated from giving unsuccessful chase to the blue car. Gigi had already retired into the pits with magneto trouble. Somewhat unexpectedly, a frustrated Alberto now handed his car, fitted with fresh sparking plugs and with a wider air intake, over to his ex-tutor.

As Enzo Ferrari later recalled: "Alberto Ascari, the driver, had a sure and precise style, but Alberto Ascari, the man, had an impelling need to get into the lead at the very beginning. When leading, he could not easily be overtaken - indeed, I will go as far as to say that it was virtually impossible to overtake him. When he was second, however, or even farther back, he had not the combative spirit I should have liked to have seen on certain occasions. This was not because he threw in the sponge; but because, when he had to get on to the tail of an adversary and pass him, he was evidently afflicted not so much by what might perhaps appear to be a sort of inferiority complex as by a state of nerves that prevented him from showing his class to the best advantage. Ascari was just the opposite of what is generally the case: usually, in fact, it is the driver in the lead who is worried - he is harrassed, he wonders whether or not he can hang on in the first place, he studies his pace and is often uncertain as to whether or not he should force it. With Alberto Ascari, though, it was exactly the contary: he felt sure of himself when he was acting as the hare, and it was at those moments that his style was seen at its superb best and no one could catch him." [1]

At Rheims, by dint of good driving, Gigi had pulled himself up to 4th place by lap 30, when he came back into the pits and handed the confused Ferrari back to Alberto. By the Finish, "Ciccio" had pulled into 3rd place, behind Farina and even set the fastest lap at 108.37 m.p.h., travelling flat-out at 150 m.p.h. between Garenne and Thillois.

[1] "Enzo Ferrari Memoirs."

But the fact remained that Frenchman, Jean Behra, in the Gordini was a potential threat to Ferrari supremacy. For the following weekend's race, new and slightly more powerful engines were fitted into the 2-liter Type 500's, as well as double magnetos to prevent overheating.

The 5th event, also the French Grand Prix proper, at Rouen-les-Essarts saw "French Favorite" Jean Behra unable to tackle the power and speed of the Italian cars. It saw a fierce Ascari-Farina duel, and then a 1st place for Alberto at 80 m.p.h., breaking the Rouen lap Record with an 84.63 m.p.h. lap. It was again noted with admiration, how Alberto took fast downhill curves, right-left-right, on full throttle, sliding rather than drifting.

July 13 was Alberto's 33rd birthday, but was also for Alberto an unlucky day-number on which to race. Event 6 in the French series took place on the acrobatic circuit of Les Sables d'Olonne on the West French Coast, near Nantes - on that very day. He began the race, was leading and had even set up the fastest lap, when Harry Schell in a Maserati-Plate (a converted 4CLT/48) put himself across the road, causing a multiple pile-up involving Ascari, Farina Cantoni and Trintignant. Alberto's car was a write-off, the race being won by Gigi Villoresi , who had picked his way round the wreckage.

The British Grand Prix at Silverstone - a week later, was a completely different sensation. Alberto got away to a stunning start, and gave an almost perfect demonstration of Grand Prix driving, playing "hare" from Start to Finish, watched by the proverbial 100,000 English spectators. Averaging 90.92 over the 2½ hours, Alberto drove those 85 laps as if on rails; calm, unhurried, self-assured.

But then, as Lampredi explains: "Engines either run well or they break down. The only characteristic of a good racing engine is that it *never* breaks down. It *never* stops. This has always been my principle, but without Alberto, that principle might never have been publicly affirmed."

From France, to England, and now back to Germany for the " Terza Volta" or "Hat-Trick" on the Nürburgring. Could he do it?

Watched by an estimated 260,000 spectators, Alberto at

once took the lead and increased it to $6\frac{1}{2}$ seconds from Dr. Farina. He was driving what he regarded as probably the finest car he'd ever driven on his favorite foreign track. By lap 4, Ascari led Farina by 59.6 seconds, helped by the latter's stopping hurriedly for fresh goggles. By lap 5, it was 69 seconds. Lesser cars were retiring one after the other. By lap 9, his lead had gone down to 45 seconds, then he made a rear-wheel-change pit stop of 32 seconds. Soon after Farina's mechanics beat this by a second, but then the Doctor spoiled it by stalling twice. Alberto seemed assured of a win.

On lap 16, Alberto came into his pit, 18 seconds behind schedule, gesticulating excitedly at the rear of the car and shoulting "Olio!" A churn of oil was flung in while he looked anxiously back down the track for the Doctor's approaching car. Ascari was still stationary when Farina roared past the pits into the lead. A determined Alberto now roared after his rival, tearing round that nightmare circuit, sliding the corners left and right, flogging the Ferrari to its limit.

A dull procession of speed had been suddenly transformed into a fierce duel - the German crowd began get excited. Farina, unruffled and grinning, fled before Ascari, but with an ever diminishing gap. The 34 year-old Milanese had re-started with 10 seconds to make up and in that one lap of 14 miles, he sliced it off to 8 at the Karussel, 7 at Wippermann, 6, at Brunchen and 4 at Swallowtail, until half-way round, he was on the 46 year-old Torinese's back. He passed in front of a roaring grandstand. Then the doctor drew level again with the car dealer as they braked for the South Curve, but Ascari deftly flung his car through a tight, sliding turn and led by a length out of the corner, going on to win by 14.1 seconds The *Ringmeister* from Italy had scored his Hat-Trick!

Seven days later, they were back in France for Event 7 of the French Series on the modified St. Gaudens Circuit at Comminges. On lap 3, Alberto mistook the course and was automatically disqualified. Eleven laps later, climbing into another works Ferrari driven by Simon, he re-entered the race, in pursuit of the Doctor By lap 16, he was two seconds *behind* Farina; by lap 28 he was 11 seconds *in front* and by lap 55, over a minute *in front.* At the Finish, Ascari was a lap ahead of

Farina, who, in turn, was five laps ahead of Jean Behra's Gordini.

This continuation of Ferrari/Ascari supremacy now took one week to travel north to a sinous little 2.6 mile circuit among the sand dunes between Haarlem City and the seaside resort of Zandvoort for the 1st official Dutch Grand Prix, presided over by Prince Bernard of the Netherlands.

Under large, black clouds and a strong cold North Sea Wind, 50,000 spectators watched eighteen cars leave the Starting Grid, amongst them, the Ferraris of Ascari, Farina and Villoresi.

Following a superlative start, Alberto piled on his lead so firmly that by lap 50, he actually lapped an astonished Gigi, and by lap 84 had lapped a very annoyed Farina. He refused to call in at the pits when the wheel change signals were put out and drove on flat-out. The Ferrari pit staff now flew out all sorts of signals to get their cars onto the same lap. Only then did Alberto slow down. Farina did a record lap of 85.26 m.p.h. and Villoresi also repassed his former pupil. Dutifully, Alberto slowed up still more, but just to be devil, did his 89th lap at a record 85.44 m.p.h., beating Farina by 0.18 m.p.h.! He crossed the Finish Line with his arm raised triumphantly, not only the victor at Zandvoort, but mathematically World Champion for 1952! He'd done it - at last!

He had won French races at Comminges, Marseilles and Rouen, so a fifth victory at La Baule on August 24th, helped to round things off as far as the French Championship series was concerned.

The final, major race, near home, was to be contested at Monza Autodrome, the track with which he had grown up - childhood, boyhood, manhood, maturity. If clinched, this race would be his 11th victory, and 6th consecutive - an achievement that would surpass all of motor-racing's legendary greats.

Rudolph Caracciola in his greatest days, gained six victories in 1935 and four in 1937. Auto Union Driver Bernd Rosemayer's best year, 1936, brought him five victories; Dick Seaman of Britain gained six "firsts" in 1936, his best year, while "Il Maestro" Tazio Nuvolari, usually recognized as the greatest of all Grand Prix road racing drivers, scored a maximum of 10 wins in one season, his best, in 1933.

But rumors now threatened to prevent this 11th victory. Omer Orsi's Maserati concern at Modena had recently recruited Colombo from Alfa-Romeo, and this engineering genius had "souped up" the lightweight A6GCM six-cylinder Maserati to give some 195 B.H.P., almost exactly equivalent to the power output of the 2-liter Ferrari.

For the Monza showdown, Orsi sent three such cars - one of them to be driven by Froilan Gonzalez, whilst Enzo Ferrari sent five cars - Ascari, Farina, Villoresi, Taruffi and Simon, Another strategic difference was that whilst the Ferraris could complete the race on one 160-liter tank, the Maseratis with their 80 liter tank, would have to stop for fuel.

September 7 was a beautiful day, blue sky stretching to behind the distant Brianza hills, with the usual crowds ready to watch 24 cars, representing 10 nationalities, compete against each other round the Lesmo and Vialone curves and along those wide straights.

The Start saw Gonzalez, that huge Argentinian "Pampas Bull" forge into the lead with his Maserati, ahead of Ascari and Villoresi, who had begun their passing and re-passing game, slipstreaming one another ahead of Farina. Gradually, Gonzalez built up his lead - 14 seconds, 19 seconds, 20 seconds, 25 seconds. Then on lap 37, the Maserati pulled into the pits to have its 80-liter tank filled up again and the two wheels changed, taking more than a minute to do so, This was far too long a pit stop. Alberto went into a lead, praying that he too would not have to make a lengthy pit stop.

Then from lap 50, another Maserati works driver, the pipe smoking Felice Bonetto, his white helmet furrowed by a red arrow, having already been lapped, started playing baulking tricks with Ascari to slow him down. This annoyed Alberto no end. Meanwhile Gonzalez had pulled himself back up from 5th, then 4th, then past Farina to 3rd, then past Villoresi to 2nd. place. But when he realized that, with only 18 laps to go, he was still 14 seconds from "Ciccio", he gave up the pursuit and eased off. Alberto finally shook himself free of Bonetto on lap 70 and finished his victory drive over the last ten laps, arriving smiling, soaked in oil and sweat, having averaged 109.97 m.p.h., with

Gigi crossing the line 30 seconds later in 2nd place.

Before he would allow a jubilant crowd to hoist him onto their shoulders, "Ciccio" had serious words with Aurelio Lampredi and Luigi Bazzi. For as Lampredi explains: "There was no need for Ascari to have full knowledge of engineering. He would either tell you 'the rear suspension seems too rigid', or 'that offside tyre seems softer than the nearside', or 'it's oversteering', or 'it's under-steering' - or sometimes, but rarely, 'this engine's going to blow up'. We'd check it out, find that nearly always he was right - and modify to correct accordingly."

'Business' over, "Ciccio" took off his gloves, swigged from a bottle of mineral water, shook hands with "Pepe" Gonzalez and embraced him as a truly equal opponent -then abandoned himself to the praise and glory that were now his - "Champion of the World", "The New Nuvolari", "The Greatest", "The Idol of Italian Motorsport". Where he had begun his career six years before as "Alberto, the son of the great Antonio Ascari", it was now "Antonio, the father of the great Alberto Ascari."

But another battle had just begun: Maserati versus Ferrari. Only one weekend later, they confronted each other for 134 miles on their home town Autodrome for the Modena Grand Prix. Although Enzo Ferrari had already spotted rising talent in the English driver, Mike Hawthorn, and had earmarked him for the 1953 season, for this race, Gigi, Alberto and Farina, now had a new teammate in young Sergio Sighinolfi. On lap 29, Ascari was leading Gonzalez by 8 seconds when the Ferrari pulled in with faulty oil circulation. Sighinolfi was flagged into the pits, climbed out and handed over to Alberto, who went off hot in pursuit, managing to pull himself up into 3rd place behind Villoresi and Gonzalez, who after a fierce duel were only fractions of a second apart.

Thus, at the end of the season, the World Championship Points Table read: Ascari 53 points; Farina 27; Taruffi 22. The Italian Championship likewise: Ascari 40 points, Farina and Taruffi 27.

Most men would have relaxed and taken it easy until the new year. Not so Gigi and Alberto, whose love of motor-racing now took them to Mexico in November for the IIIrd Carrera Pan Americana with a 4.1 liter Ferrari sportscar. On the first leg of that long distance road race, the 530 Km of Tuxtla-Gutierrez-Oaxaca, Alberto was in the lead from 90 other cars, travelling a 105 m.p.h Anticipating a right curve over a hill, he found a sharper left instead. The Ferrari sportscar rocketed up the wall of a cut, rolled and skidded hundreds of meters down the road on its fragile alloy roof. Luckily for Alberto, that car was a coupé.

For two months, Alberto Ascari could now return home to Number 60, Corso Sempione, to Mietta his wife, to 10 year old Tonino and 8 year-old Patrizia, to his long-suffering mother, Eliza. He could spend Christmas and see in the New Year as every family man, father and husband should - and take a much needed rest from that travelling Grand Prix circus, for which at present, he was the star performer.

"A Shadow Of Self"

What were the individual facets which made up the personality of the man known as Alberto Ascari - and what was he like away from motorsport? It seems that he regulated every facet of his behavior so as to maintain his nervous system at its most balanced.

His close friend, Gilberto Colombo explains: "Alberto was extremely interesting as a character - objective, reflective, very calm and serene. Not for one single second do I recall his having done anything to complicate our friendship. Whoever was with Alberto Ascari always felt at ease. If there were complications, he wanted to know the opinions of others, obtaining them quietly. His handwriting was upright and angular, with no complicated flourishes or loops."

His wife, Mietta, recalls: "Alberto was a robust, rosy-faced man, a very light-hearted, jovial character, an extrovert who attracted people, made merry with them and knew how to laugh heartily and joyfully. Cameraderie. Yet he could be rather prudish at times; he did not enjoy telling jokes, he cringed when I told them, and it annoyed him when other people cursed or swore or tried to tell dirty stories. He had a soft and deep voice, and as someone born and bred in Milan, he was fluent in our local city dialect, 'meneghino'.

Fully aware of the anxiety he was causing both his mother and wife, he always went out of his way to 'undramatize' his life keeping utterly calm, always maintaining that he personally considered motor racing as nothing more than his trade and that he might just as well have been the head-waiter of an expensive restaurant.

Although a bronze bust of Antonio Ascari on a simple wooden plinth stood in the entrance hall of Corso Sempione 60, erected by a thoughtful son to the memory of an unforgettable father, daylight was excluded from that hall, the bust standing there in semi-darkness. Upstairs in the flat, cups, trophies and relics of all kinds were carefully hidden in a discreet, crystal cabinet.

Mietta continues: "At home, one did not speak about motor racing. When he was away racing, he often telephoned me, but we chatted about banal things, about the children, the weather, about whether I was going out or staying in - for he became very jealous of me when he was not at home; he would ring me in the evenings, at midnight even, so I could never go out. I went out dancing with him, but never when he was away.

"Sometimes I would go and watch him race, but other times I would stay in Milan. When I waited at home, that telephone became a terrible thing. To ease the tension, I would either play cards with my friends, or go out to the cinema with a female friend, because during those two hours, I was not thinking about him motor-racing, risking his life. I didn't want the children around me during these hours, because I was very agitated and preferred that they went out to the Park with their nurse, to be happy and playful. That is, I wanted to be free to be nervous, sad or whatever, without having to hide it from them.

"Sometimes I would listen to Italian Radio (RAI) for the sporting results. But if Alberto had had some accident, or had retired, or not been in the first 3 places, I did not know. So I telephoned the Sports Desk of Italian Radio and asked them for information. Sometimes they knew, sometimes they did not. Then I had to wait for his telephone call. If, on the other hand, I heard that he had arrived 1st, 2nd or 3rd, I calmed down and smoked a cigarette.

"When he returned, I also knew what had happened by his mood. If everything had gone well, you could see it on his face. Otherwise he was nervous because something had forced him to retire - or he'd had a disagreement with another driver. Sometimes there was no need for words. Sometimes I asked him. But usually, on entering our flat, it had become of secondary importance. There were family problems and races were another issue.

"When he returned from abroad, he would bring back precious and semi-precious stones, saying 'Fur coats will lose their value. These won't'. For the children from Germany came mechanical toys and toy cars for Tonino, whilst at Rheims at France, they made special dolls, in a different costume each year, for him to bring back to Patrizia.

"I was more strict with the children than he was, because he was at home, which was seldom, he gave them everything they wanted; then he went off again and I would have to regain control of them. They called him 'Ciccio' as well as 'Papa'. But neither Tonino nor Patrizia ever went to see their father race."

In Alberto's own words, "I usually try to give my children everything they need - even if it is only to satisfy a whim. All the same, though, I think it as well that I should be severe with them: I don't want them to get too fond of me. One of these days I may not come back - and they will suffer less if I have kept them at arm's length."

Mietta continues "Although we could exclude motor-racing as a topic of conversation, inevitably his fame pursued him into our private life. Wherever we went, the 'tifosi' (fans and admirers) would pester him for his autograph. We received thousands of letters, fanmail, among them people asking for money, cars, help - many people wrote, asking him to teach them to drive! Every so often we had to throw literally boxfuls of fanmail away - but there was also one day in the year when Alberto, who in his own quiet way had an extremely generous nature, said to me, 'Now we'll do something about these letters' and we'd deal with several of them to the extent that we were able. But he didn't like people taking advantage of his friendship, who only wanted to meet him so that they could say they were 'friends' with the great Alberto Ascari'. He hated journalists who pestered him, interviewed him and then went away and wrote what they wanted."

Gilberto Colombo remembers Alberto saying to him, 'I have never put myself at the wheel of a car when I am tired.' "He never fixed the time of our departure for an ordinary journey. So we have to do 500 Km and be there by this evening. 'Look Gilberto' he'd say. 'I'm going to get up when I feel rested and no longer feel tired. When I'm ready, I'll telephone you, we'll have a chat and then we'll leave.' He never tried anything when he was not up to it. When crossing a city, he drove calmly and respectfully, always on the look-out for wobbling cyclists or careless pedestrians. He himself was the model pedestrian and always did his kerb-drill. Once on the autostrada or national routes, he went extremely fast, but engendered in his passenger sense of absolute security. He often changed his personal car, saying that a car must always be new and well-kept. I think that my friend, Alberto Ascari, realized that as a World Champion, it was his duty to be an exemplary Italian citizen. I even remember his making a broadcast about road safety on the newly-born Italian television."

Mietta: "When Alberto was in training, which was usually eleven out of twelve months in the year, he kept to an extremely healthy routine. Although he was a 'bon gustaio', a great lover of food - pasta ascuitta, rissotto alla Milanese, French cheeses and patés, German wursts - his favorite food was beefsteak, done 'rare' , with eggs and a normal salad. He did not like curries and hot, spicy dishes, and prefered a good wholesome wine to an inebriating 'short'. He hardly ever smoked.

"He would, if possible, get up late, and take his time to wash, shave and dress, which he did - as he did most things - very meticulously.

"We were among the first Italians to have a television set, and after that arrived, he never again went out to the cinema, theater or shows. Indeed every evening, we had people come round to our apartment, just to watch this novelty. I was always serving drinks, while they just watched. Becoming a 'waitress' for television zombies, rather annoyed me!"

"Every night he went to bed at 10.30, glanced at the newspapers, and at exactly 11 o'clock he would fall asleep. I once referred to him as a methodical, bourgeois husband. But it was only when he stubbed his foot on his trainer-bicycle in our bedroom that he cured himself of sleep-walking.

"For his daily exercise, he would do gymnastics and 'footing' (fast, athletic walking) round the Velodromo Vigorelli, a small bicycle arena near Corso Sempione. With this conscientious preparation, he had an almost perfect physique.

"Often, before he left for Argentina, we would go to Cortina d'Ampezzo and enjoy some snow-skiing. Then when he was in Belgium, he and Nino Farina would play golf with King Beaudoin, and ex-King Leopold, who were Ferrari enthusiasts - and when they came to Italy, there would be the return match either at Monza, or Rapallo golfcourse."

"In the summer months, we had a flat down at Santa Margherita di Liguria, on the Riviera, near Genoa, where Alberto, who suffered from hay fever, could get away from the grass and tree pollen, and go swimming and rowing and sunbathing to his heart's content.

Alberto was a good Catholic and went to Church every Sunday,where he would light a candle, not to St. Alberto, but to St. Antonio of Padua - and not without reason. Ferdinand Martin de Bulloens was born on 15 August 1195 in Lisbon, Portugal. When he died, on Friday 13 June 1232, Brother Antonio of Padua was two months short of his 37th birthday. Alberto's father, Antonio, had died just two months short of his 37th birthday. In Italian folklore, St. Antonio had become known as the saint of the lily. He was patron of thirteen things and could give thirteen pardons. In the Italian region of Abruzzi, to obtain something from him, it was necessary to recite, thirteen times, in silence, the prayer:

"Sand'Andonie di Paduve
Che dde Paduve aveniste
Tridece grazij a Ddi' cerchiste
Tutt'a ttridece 'aveste
Facete 'na grazij a mme,
Pe' le cinghe piaghe de Ggesu Criste"

It became extremely common in churches and other places of devotion, to celebrate bread collections for St. Antonio; but bread in the Puglia region, was prepared in thirteen loaves, to divide among the poor, with flour obtained from the first grain of the year; otherwise with that obtained from sheaves of ears of corn which had been blessed and which were offered up to the saint at harvest-time. Among prayers said were the "Pater, Ave and Gloria", thirteen times in the name of the saint - this to be done once a day for one hundred days! Similarly in 1898, Pope Leo XIII granted to the faithful who, on thirteen successive Tuesdays, or as many successive Sundays, should spend some time in pious meditation - a Plenary Indulgence. And so it went on. Therefore, for Alberto, the religious association with that particular saint appeared to be almost a numerological one.

"Not that we escaped from his superstition even there. One

day, during a terrible Mediterranean storm, he was driving us back to the flat by our usual route. Five minutes and we would have been there. But then a cat crossed the road.. we made a complete tour of the mountain, a much longer route, just to go home! There was nothing that could be done about it.

"Alberto made friends with other Italian sportsmen - Fausto Coppi, the legendary cycling champion; Mario Verga, the motorboat-racing champion. We spent some most enjoyable days up alongside Lake Como with Mario and Liliana Verga."

Alberto had this to say of himself: "People have often asked me if I am not haunted by the thought of the tragic destiny of my father - whether I am not tormented by the obsession of one day finishing up like him. No, I hardly ever think of it, nor do I ask myself whether it is fair as regards my mother, my wife and my children - or even myself. Look, I am risking my life thousands of times to pursue victory around the world. Like my father, like all those who embrace this career, I only obey my instinct: without it, I would not know how to live, I would not succeed in making any sense of my days. Every race driver, after a time, gets used to risk and thinks no more about it; and then during a contest, you are so determined to win that you only think of passing your competitors and coming first at the Finish. I am a great admirer of "Faust" and the courage with which he has known how to react to misfortune; this opera is a beautiful demonstration of strength of character."

"To Win At Will"

Before long, family concerns again gave way to a new ambition: In defending his World Title in 1953, Alberto would be achieving what Farina, then Fangio had failed to do. It would not be easy though, for now Fangio was attempting to make a come-back as part of a redoutable four-man Maserati works team, also taking in Gonzalez, Bonetto and Marimon. For company, Alberto would again be joined by Gigi and Farina, but also by the promising new Englishman from Farnham, Surrey - the blonde, Mike Hawthorn.

Lampredi recalls: "We invited Hawthorn to come to Modena to test our car. He arrived with his own car, went round Modena autodrome in his own car, then went round in ours. Having accustomed himself to ours, he tried his again, left the track and ended up in hospital for a month. After that he stayed with us."

Although the Argentine Grand Prix on January 18 1953 saw a victorious Ascari, followed by Villoresi in 2nd place and Gonzalez 3rd - it also showed an uncertain Fangio that he had not lost his touch, despite his Maserati breaking down. Two weeks later, while Ascari retired in the Buenos Aires Grand Prix on General Peron's new Argentinian Autodrome, at least Fangio was placed 9th. Farina won that race from Villoresi and Hawthorn - a Ferrari benefit.

The first major European race took place at Pau on April 7, under a cloudy and threatening sky; three hours of racing watched by 20,000 people and Ferrari making sure of a sound victory. Alberto's fastest time in practice was 1'39"2, whilst Farina's 1'39"3, - the difference, a tenth of a second! The only time that Farina threatened him in the race itself came on lap 2 when the Doctor was for a moment in the lead. But when he spun off on lap 33, Alberto had the 72 remaining laps of the race to himself, breaking his own lap record, set in 1951, and becoming the first man to average over 100 Km/h during a race at Pau. Mike Hawthorn came in 2nd, just over a mile behind.

One hundred miles north of Pau. exactly one month later, another French race - the Bordeaux Grand Prix - racing round a 2.5. Km circuit in a town famous for its red wine, the red Ferraris again showed their mettle. Watched by 60,000 spectators, sixteen cars started - among them a blue Gordini driven by Fangio, cheered on by the partisan French. Ascari led from start to finish of the 123-lap race with Villoresi and Farina at his back: after only one-third of the race, Alberto had already lapped eleven competitors out of fifteen, including a cautious Fangio.

The Ferrari team now split forces. Hawthorn went home to England and won the Silverstone International Trophy, whilst Farina, Villoresi and Ascari went down to Naples for a battle with the new Maseratis of Fangio and Gonzalez. Alberto had been leading Fangio by 8 seconds at lap 23 when the support for the accelerator pedal broke and he went into the pits for repairs. He lost 2 laps. The race was won by Farina, followed by Fangio, Gonzalez and Villoresi - and then in 5th place, Alberto who had re-entered the race following hasty repairs. This result definitely showed the Maseratis as a force to be reckoned with.

On March 20, Alberto received a letter from Ernest I. Ruiz, of Modesto, California, offering him the chance to drive a Kurtis Kraft car in the "Indianapolis"500" - in other words, a powerful car, custom-built for "brickyard-style" racing. Although Alberto's greatest ambition was to go back and win Indy, he would not accept, because he still retained the hope the Ferrari would make an Italian car ready for him. As it is, he never did, Alberto never went, and Bill Vukovitch won the 1953 race, driving a Kurtis Kraft car.

Three weeks later, Fangio driving a V-16 BRM, came back on form and, much to Alberto's consternation, the Argentinian gave the Italian a run for his money at the Albi Grand Prix, a Formula One race in two heats. Heat One: Fangio won when Alberto, having in vain tried to outdo him, retired to the pits with a long trail of oil from a smoking engine - gearbox trouble. Heat Two: Fangio retired with mechanical trouble.

But Championship racing in 1953 and the Ferrari-Maserati

duel began in earnest at Zandvoort with the Dutch Grand Prix.

Aurelio Lampredi recalls: "We had four Ferraris, exactly the same, and Ascari was going much faster in practice than Farina. So Farina was complaining that his car was not as good as Ascari's, that the gears were inferior. During the night, we dismantled the gears and did everything we could to show the Doctor that both cars were the same. Then Ascari asked Farina: 'By the way, on that bend X, which gear did you select?' 'Well, er, on that bend I selected 4th'

'Me too!'

'And on bend Y, I chose 3rd - '

'Me too!'

'So?'

'So!'

June 7. Race Day. Four Maseratis are being lined up on the Zandvoort Starting Grid against four Ferraris. Alberto is chatting to Farina "I've never seen you looking so well. Today it will be difficult to keep you behind!"

"I would prefer that it will be difficult for you to keep in front of me", answers Farina, smiling, and with a routine gesture, he passes a finger under the collar of his vest. It is then that the face of Farina changes: he suddenly stops smiling; on his scarred forehead a deep frown.

"What's up?" asks Ascari. Farina suddenly turns his back on his colleague and runs off. There is only one quarter of an hour before the Start. Farina returns just in time to climb in make the Start.

The track had only been surfaced a week before, with the result that - apart from the sand from the dunes, the gravel top surface was loose. So instead of the spray of a rainy day peppering the drivers' faces like pin-pricks, grit, resembling chips of ice, jabbed at them as well, and they had a hard time preventing their cars from snaking and sliding.

Despite this, Alberto, in his immaculately regular style, once described as "like a rapid utensil that cuts steel with a micrometric precision and an acute, tranquil, deliberation which contrasts against the ruthless, aggressive action of Farina" - went into a lead that he kept until the end of the 90th and Final. He averaged 80.99 m.p.h., followed by Farina, and then by Froilan Gonzalez in the Maserati who became the hero of the day in his make-or-break chasing and finally overtaking, Mike Hawthorn for 3rd place. Alberto drove so well that by lap 15 he already had the tail-enders in sight; indeed, halfway through the race, spectators realising the result was a foregone conclusion began to disperse. Gigi clocked the fastest lap at 83.1 m.p.h. and then was forced to retire.

That evening, during the honorary dinner, Alberto was finally able to ask Farina what had been the matter: The Doctor explained that he had left a little gold medal on his wash-basin; the medal showing the smiling Madonna della Consiliata, a medal he had worn about his neck since, aged only 17 years, he had competed in his first race, fifteen years before.

"It's far easier to forget something like this than your blue helmet, Alberto", said the Doctor intensely.

The Maserati challenge progressed one stage further a few days later in the Belgian Grand Prix at Spa-Francorchamps. Not only did Fangio unofficially break the lap record in practice, a record not bettered during the race itself, but for the first ten laps of this extremely fast circuit, Gonzalez, followed by Fangio were actually leading the Ferraris, gradually building up a considerable advantage. On lap 11, Gonzalez retired with a broken accelerator pedal on his Maserati, while Fangio led Ascari by 34 seconds and Farina by 54. This was looking to be Fangio's race, but then two laps later he was forced in with an over-heated Maserati engine, and the Ferraris went into the lead - Alberto, then Gigi.

Belgian Johnny Claes was now made to hand over *his* Maserati to Fangio who went off in pursuit some 2½ minutes behind Alberto. No way could he make up such a distance by the end of the race, but Fangio was determined to remind himself of his old ability. Climbing up past competitor after competitor, the brave Argentinian had soon closed that lead down to 27 seconds with three laps from the end, then 23 seconds - then on the Stavelot Corner, he skidded on a patch of oil, his Maserati went off the road, rolling over and over on the grass, having thrown out its driver who, this time, was unhurt.

Having averaged 112.47 m.p.h. for 2 hours, 48 minutes 30

seconds, Alberto made excuses for his "fluffed" start by saying "I realized that if I played the waiting game, the Maseratis would soon overdo it."

One week later, Alberto was back in Italy and driving a 2.5. liter Ferrari sportscar in the Autodrome Grand Prix. During practice, he had noticed that the brake on the Ferrari was too short - so he had it lengthened a little. During the race he was leading when that brake pedal bent itself over the accelerator pedal with the result that, as he entered the Lesmo corner on the 13th lap, when he pushed down what he *thought* was the brake, instead of slowing, it increased the speed and he hit another car, the Berlinetta of Signora Piazza, in the back and the Ferrari went off the track.

"I didn't know exactly what had happened; I distinctly remember only that the car, going through the bushes, moved zigzag for 60 meters, jumping up and hitting the shrubs. Next thing, I found myself standing up. My first reaction was to shake arms, legs and feel my thorax to persuade myself that I was whole. No injuries at all. I ran towards the boxes to First Aid. Friends who had witnessed the accident told me that they had literally seen me flying out of the car and falling heavily on the soil. Personally, on reflection, I had the impression of being seated up to the last moment in my seat and of coming out of my car when it stopped. But the film of that race showed my car after the accident, upturned, wheels in the air - proving my friends to be right."

The show-down - O. K. Corral style - or in other words the Trident of Maserati versus the Prancing Horse of Ferrari, finally came, one week later, in what has been described as one of *the* greatest and most closely fought races of all time. The venue was Rheims and the French Grand Prix.

By now, it was known that while the Maserati had the higher top speed, the Ferrari had more usable power "low down" and better road-holding. Scuderia Ferrari entered Ascari, Villoresi, Farina and Hawthorn. Officine Maserati opposed them with Fangio, Gonzalez, Marimon and Bonetto. There were seventeen other cars in the race, including a British Cooper-Alta driven by a young Stirling Moss.

Alberto set the fastest lap in practice at 115.83 m.p.h., but then the other Ferraris and Maseratis did not vary more than 3 seconds slower than that - suggesting a close race.

But just how extremely close, nobody could ever have imagined. At flag-fall, Bonetto shot ahead of both Ascari and Villoresi in the front row of the Grid, so that Gonzalez, with half-full tanks in an accordingly lighter Maserati, roared into the lead, pursued by a snaking line of cars as if "on tow": Ascari (2.8 seconds down), Villoresi, Bonetto, Fangio, Hawthorn, Farina and Marimon just five seconds behind - or in other words, Maserati, Ferrari, Ferrari, Maserati, Maserati, Ferrari, Ferrari, Maserati.

Gonzalez, crouched down as much as his burly frame would let him in his cockpit, now acclerelated away up to 20 seconds in front of a tight bunch of four Ferraris, followed by Fangio and his Argentinian protégé Onofre Marimon in their Maseratis, whilst Felice Bonetto spun at Thillois and dropped back to 9th place. Alberto and Gigi had now taken to playing the passing and re-passing game with Mike Hawthorn. During those first 20 laps, Alberto led on 11 laps, Mike on 6 and Gigi on 2.

Lap 23: Fangio "said goodbye" to his protégé Marimon and went off to overtake Farina. Lap 24: Farina re-took Fangio. Then Fangio put in a lap at 115.84 m.p.h. and pulled himself past Farina, Villoresi and Ascari into 3rd place. Lap 29: Gonzalez stopped for fuel, lost his lead, took only 27 seconds and came back in 5th place.

Fangio now took a lead of half a second from Hawthorn, with Alberto 3rd 0.4. seconds behind and Farina just 6 seconds behind in 4th place. Fangio held that lead for two laps, then Hawthorn led for three. Passing and re-passing, intense, lap after lap, nose-to-tail, hub-cap to hub-cap; Maserati using its top-speed advantage to the limit, Ferrari cornering with superb road holding and initial acceleration. The lap times of Mike Hawthorn and Juan Manuel Fangio showed a variance of only a few seconds. Fangio used every subtle trick that he knew to shake off the tenacious Englishman - but it was a game of magnets.

Meanwhile, "The Pampas Bull" had driven furiously and, overtaking Farina, now engaged in a separate 3rd/4th place duel with Alberto, leaving the Doctor in 5th place, while Marimon and Villoresi dropped back.

And so it went on - Fangio and Hawthorn swapping furiously for 1st place, Ascari and Gonzalez swapping furiously for 3rd place. It was often a question of *less* than the length of a red Italian racing car.

With two laps to go, two pairs of cars crossed the line less than one second apart - each pair absolutely level - Ferrari-Maserati, Ferrari-Maserati. Never before had such a desperate high-speed struggle been waged on a Grand Prix circuit!

The Finish was a 140 m.p.h. crescendo. To the wild cheering and clapping of a huge holiday crowd, Mike Hawthorn tactically outsmarted Fangio by using the better condition of his Ferrari's brakes and letting the Argentinian lead into that very last corner - then using the Maserati's slipstream to accelerate the Ferrari first over the line, precisely one hairsbreadth of a second ahead. Gonzalez got alongside Fangio just before the Finish but was pipped to the post by 0.4. of a second and Heaven only knows how many centimeters of car; Alberto came in 4th, three seconds later - then Farina and Villoresi a minute behind. The first four cars had been separated by a mere 4.6. seconds.

A frenzied crowd went berserk, as everyone, proclaiming him as the new ace, including an admiring Fangio, congratulated the 24 year-old Mike Hawthorn, the third British driver ever to win the French Grand Prix, nicknaming him "Papillon" ("Butterfly") for the polka-dot bow tie the Englishman sported throughout the race.

The point score for the 1953 World Title now stood at Ascari 28; Hawthorn 14; Villoresi 13; Gonzalez 12.

The Maseratis had nearly toppled the Ferraris on French soil. Two weeks passed as those sleek red monsters and their highly experienced ace-drivers went north across the channel to English soil and up to Silverstone to re-engage combat at the British Grand Prix on July 18.

On the unlucky July 17, enter one black cat... as Alberto later reported: "Several days before the race, I went to a hotel in Northampton. One morning, I discovered, with fright, a black cat quietly positioned on the landing outside my bedroom. 'God knows what's going to happen to me now! I thought. Punctually, every morning, right up until the day of the race, which took place on Saturday, the cat could be found in front of my door. . ."

Threatening weather did not prevent huge crowds from turning up that day to see whether the Trident of Modena could make a more successful plunge at the Prancing Horse of Maranello, and to see whether the "Farnham Flyer", Hawthorn could repeat his Rheims sensation on home territory.

They also came to see the Silverstone favorites - "Ciccio" Ascari and Gigi Villoresi, who had come to be regarded as perennial attractions - the popular, English cult of the sleek red Italian Ferraris...

One of the most fascinating sights for anyone near the pits was to see the pudgy Alberto and the silver haired Gigi before the Start of a race. While all around them, other drivers were pulling on and off their gloves, adjusting their goggles and giving all the signs of being thoroughly keyed up, the Italian duo remained cool and calm - indolent almost, chatting and smiling, even lying back on the straw bales to relax. But the minute Alberto Ascari climbed into that car, that indolence completely disappeared. For, as Gigi explains:

"When he put those goggles over his eyes, they suddenly became as cold as steel, intense, concentrated. They were no longer the eyes of the 'Ciccio' Ascari of several minutes before. For he had now entered into the life of that race, and everything that race represented. Because, look, in those final two minutes, you see your whole life - past, present, future -flash in front of you, including the things that can go wrong. Not with fear, because you would not be able to race - but with a tough, logical self-control."

It might seem that to make a good start, a driver must race off as soon as he saw the flag fall. It was not that easy. Some looked at the finger muscles of the hand of the man with the flag, going off when those muscles clenched. Others looked at his chest muscles, which would swell out as he took a breath before dropping the flag. Alberto Ascari had a sixth sense for starting combined with the perfect of minimal amount of wheelspin and maximum drive - and, as Gigi explains, something else on his side:

"Justly, Alberto for Ferrari became Number One, both in his ability and with the friendship they had. They were very close,

Alberto regarding Ferrari almost like a father and becoming something of a 'spoilt child'. This was then transmitted by Ferrari to his subordinates, such as Nello Ugolini, to whose son, Alberto became godfather. One of the secrets of a good start was to be considered as Number One."

True to form, he was superbly away in this race. Never having had a lead to "play himself" into the first couple of laps, he at once started lapping at 89.28 m.p.h., going past, one, two and three seconds ahead of the Maseratis of Fangio and Gonzalez then, Villoresi.

Lap 2: Mike Hawthorn's Ferrari, travelling at 100 m.p.h., made one of the most monumental double-spins ever seen at Silverstone, crashing through the fence onto the grass carving up turf and mud like a mechanical scythe. Amazingly, he found his way back onto the track and continued the race.

Meanwhile, Alberto, at the steady rate of a second per lap, increased his lead to 10 seconds. Then Gonzalez's Maserati overfull with oil, started depositing the surplus round the track and lap 12, causing many other drivers a very greasy time. Following frantic and, at first, futile efforts to flag Gonzalez in, the huge Argentinian finally stopped at the pits. When the stream of Spanish abuse had subsided and he rejoined the race, "Pepe" had fallen back to 7th place; but with a typical Latin American *furora,* by lap 20 he had overtaken Hawthorn, Marimon and Farina.

Unable to make use of their Maserati's top-speed advantage, neither Fangio nor Gonzalez could make any impression on Alberto, who by lap 40, making it all look so easy, was leading by 18 seconds on Fangio, whilst Gigi in 3rd place was leading Gonzalez by a minute; young Marimon and Dr. Farina were battling it out behind.

Lap 56: Gigi's back axle gave way and a silver-haired figure was seen strolling away from the stranded Ferrari, slipping off his gloves in calm resignation. Meanwhile Ascari and Fangio duelled for 1st, Gonzalez and Farina for 3rd. Although it was not a shade on Rheims, it was still Maserati 2nd. Alberto was faultless and driving at the very peak of his form "a hard man to beat" as Fangio was to recall many years later. Lap 50: 36 seconds ahead of Fangio. Lap 75: 44 seconds ahead. The remaining fifteen laps were completed under a thunderstorm and a violent downpour of rain. As he crossed the Finish Line, 60 seconds ahead of Fangio, the checkered flag came off its baton and symbolically wrapped itself around the Ferrari's radiator cowl. It was Alberto Ascari's 4th English victory on the famous circuit. And as for that black cat...? Perhaps black cats brought *good* luck in England. He had averaged 92.97 m.p.h. against Fangio's 92.43 m.p.h.

Alberto spoke only a few words of English, yet he often confessed to his great liking for Britain and the British.

But then his typically non-Italian temperament was more akin to the calm, British, stiff upper-lip. His wife, Mietta, once compared him to John Wayne in his coolness. He once confessed that it was a matter of great regret to him that the British Grand Prix was not held later in the season so that he could stay for one month.

But within the week following the Silverstone victory, he was back at Spa in Belgium, co-driving with Gigi a 4.5. liter Ferrari sportscar in the 24-hour race. When in the 17th hour, while leading, their back axle broke, Farina and Hawthorn went into a lead they kept until 7 hours later and victory.

Conveniently, Spa was literally 50 miles west and one weekend away from the next performance of the Ferrari-Maserati circus, namely the Nürburgring. Alberto Ascari, triple *Ringmeister,* Europe's "Fastest Gun" must now defend his title in the Eifel Mountains.

The XlVth Grosser Preis von Deutschland was watched in rainy conditions by a vast crowd arrived from West Germany, Holland and Belgium. Alberto, who had set up the fastest lap in practice was pole man on the front of the Grid, alongside Fangio, Farina and Hawthorn. 2nd row: Bonetto, Villoresi and Trintignant. Gonzalez had injured himself driving a Lancia sportscar in the Portuguese Grand Prix and so was absent. Among the other competing cars, Gordinis, Connaughts, Coopers, Veritas, AFMs etc.

For once, Ascari did not lead straight away - instead, Fangio with Ascari, Hawthorn and Bonetto on his tail. But Alberto soon elbowed past and completed lap 1 with 11 seconds' advantage on the Argentinian, followed by Hawthorn, Farina, Villoresi, Bonetto etc.

By lap 3, Hawthorn and Fangio had begun a Rheims-type duel - but this time, 37 seconds behind Ascari. It looked like the Hat-Trick-plus-one for the man from Milan. But then, on lap 5, Alberto had an accident that was to put him into 9th place. Near the so-called "Oak Tree of St. Anthony", he had been travelling at around 145 m.p.h., when the offside front wheel had departed! Justly So. But I would not have accepted it in other races."

In $6\frac{1}{2}$ seconds, Alberto was in the cockpit and off like a scalded cat; driving meteorically, he created a new Formula 2 lap record on lap 12 and by lap 14, had third man Hawthorn in sight. Could he pull himself up into 1st? He must get some sort of placing or he would drop down the World Champ-ionship Points Table.

But then further misfortune dogged him and as the Ferrari crackled past the pits, there was a loud clatter and it went out of sight with blue smoke pouring from the bonnet. Reluctantly he slowed, Bonetto's Maserati passing into 4th place. After an unduly long time, he came into the pits with a burst engine. He quietly packed his light-blue helmet and goggles into his bag, put on his customary tweed-type sportscoat, and walked away from the pit to a spontaneous ovation for a man who had tried harder than he had ever tried before - and lost, ringing in his ears.

The race continued to the Finish, Farina's Ferrari leading Fangio's Maserati, suffering from a broken exhaust pipe, by a minute, with Hawthorn half a minute behind. Interestingly, Gigi managed to nurse Alberto's discarded Ferrari up into 8th place.

He had failed in France and failed in Germany. Farina and Hawthorn now threatened his World Title. Three weeks later he was given another chance to further increase his points total - the Swiss Grand Prix on the Bremgarten Circuit, outside Berne. This 4.25 mile course was a driver's circuit, made up of private and public roads, tarmac and cobblestone, with hardly any slow corners or fast straights. Bremgarten circuit wound backwards and forwards, uphill and downhill; a driver dazzled by the glare of the sun would suddenly find himself going through the darkness of a forest. In short, a circuit difficult to master.

On August 23, 70,000 people turned up on the outskirts of Berne to expect another Maserati-Ferrari scrap. Following the Start, Fangio, having swapped for better cars with Bonetto, had retired with tyre trouble on lap 10 and rejoined the fray too far behind to catch up; but catch up he had tried to do, doing one lap at 100 m.p.h., only to retire on lap 30, when one of the pistons of his Maserati burned out.

Alberto was leading, had spaced himself over half a minute in front of Farina, Hawthorn and Villoresi, when on lap 39, following an ominous mis-fire, he came into the pits with carburettor trouble. He was out for the next 13 laps, losing $87\frac{1}{2}$ seconds, during which time Onofre Marimon's Maserati suffered rear axle failure and he retired: Gigi's Ferrari smashed against the palisades, denting its nose, and also the steering connections. Back in the pits, after some frantic bashing with a mallet, he re-joined the race in 6th place.

The carburettor fixed, Alberto went off in one of his inimitable pursuits of Farina and Hawthorn. By lap 50 he had reduced Farina's lead down to 25 seconds! But then, with fifteen laps to go, pit manager Ugolini showed the hold position to his three Ferrari drivers. This was completely ignored by Alberto, who passed Hawthorn on lap 52 and went sailing past Farina to resume his lead on lap 54. Dazzled by the sun, Alberto Ascari received the checkered flag on the 65th and final lap, with a sigh of relief. He had not only averaged 97.10 m.p.h., but had beaten Bernd Rosemeyer's long-standing record for the Swiss circuit which had stood since 1937 with the Union.

He had only just climbed out of his car, when an infuriated Dr. Farina came at him with a torrent of abuse, telling off his team-mate for dis-regarding pit signals. Alberto merely shrugged and pointed out that the Swiss victory had given him his second World Championship, and marched off in high dudgeon. Ascari was left to explain to Ugolini just why he had chosen to ignore pit signals, and explained, rather lamely that the sun was in his eyes as he approached the pit area. Farina never really forgave Ascari for that incident.

But the fact remained that Alberto Ascari *was* World

Champion again - 1952 and 1953 - with 47 points, against Farina's 26, Hawthorn's 26 and Fangio's 19.

During the week that followed, a smoldering Farina refused to speak to Ascari as they journeyed back to the Nürburgring to co-drive, as prearranged, a 4.5. liter Ferrari open sportscar in the One Thousand Kilometers Race (620.7 miles). 53 cars started this gruelling 44-lap race. Only 27 finished. Ascari and Farina won the race in 8 hours 20 minutes 44 seconds at an average 74.7 m.p.h. The ice was broken by a joint victory. Farina was considerably mollified, but still far from friendly. Soon after, this, Enzo Ferrari announced that he was going to retire from motor-racing. He was thoroughly fed-up with getting no subsidy for his racing from either the Italian Government or the motor industry and was determined to pull out unless something tangible was done.

In the shadow of this news, the XXIVth Gran Premio d'Italia was held at Monza on September 13th. The twisting circuits of Silverstone, the Nürburgring and Bremgarten had never allowed the Maseratis to use the full advantage of top-speed acceleration and they suffered under the superior road-holding of their rival Ferraris. But with the expansive Monza Autodrome, there was more of a chance of equal footing.

Ascari, Farina, Hawthorn, Villoresi versus Fangio and Marimon. It was again a tremendous struggle. Three World Champions battling it out, alternating in the first three places from Start to Finish, never yielding an inch; ability, experience, bravery and determination fused into maximum effort.

In the first half of that 80 lap race, the lead position changed 14 times and 10 times in the second half. Farina led on 9 laps, Fangio on 12 laps and Ascari on 59 laps. They were taking it in turns to lead at speeds over 110 m.p.h., never more than 2 seconds apart, nose-to-tail or abreast, with the front wheel of one car tucked in beside another driver's elbow; hubcap bumped with hub-cap, spokes were fragile, but Fangio trusted Ascari's skill as a driver to allow for such events.

The muscular, precise Fangio with his brown, peaked helmet; the wiry, lean, ruthless, temperamental Farina with his white peaked helmet and the pudgy, shrewd, unflurried Ascari with his blue peakless, motorcycling helmet - seemed to merge into one, shimmering, triple-engined red, racing-car, cheered on by hysterically excited Italian fans.

It continued like this until lap 79, then the final lap saw a complete reversal of fortunes. Onofre Marimon, having been lapped several times in his Maserati, - whether deliberately or not - had become caught up in this brilliant trio. Just one kilometer from the finish, on the final (Vedano) bend, Alberto seemed on the curve to victory, when he came across another lapped, slower, car. If he had braked, Farina and Fangio, those few meters behind would have passed him.

"I decided to throw myself towards the outside of the track. The opening was very narrow. In a flash, I saw clearly that I would not succeed in passing. But I wanted to risk it despite everything. When you race 500 Km as important as Monza and are so close to success, it is impossible to hesistate in front of danger. It is perhaps a madness, a useless risk, but one feels the right and almost the duty to try. So, at 105 m.p.h. I attempted the narrow outside passage. At this point the track was streaked with oil, my Ferrari skidded sidways. Farina, just behind me, braked and swerved: he lost precious time and Fangio who was 3rd, succeeded in sliding between us and winning.

"I had never lost a race in the final meters. It's a thing that stings, especially if you think that I had led the race for the last 27 laps, and previously for another 32. But then it *was* the 13th of the month."

Such were Ascari's recollections - interesting when compared to those of Fangio: ". . . all Ascari could do was to slam on his brakes, throwing his car across the track. Behind him Marimon was coming up like a cannon-ball. I was less than three feet away when I heard the metallic crash of the collision. Meanwhile, beyond the little group, Farina courageously drove off the track to avoid hitting them. We were all in a tight bunch. I gripped the wheel, desperately steering to my right on the inside of the corner. Before me loomed the menace of slower cars which, had it been a straight, were perfectly lined up for passing.

"I still do not know how I found my way through that mess as Ascari's spin threw up a cloud of dust. I picked up speed

126

again and flashed towards the Finish Line. Farina, calmly back on the track, trailed me by a few hundred meters. Villoresi came in Third, followed by Hawthorn, Trintignant and Mieres."

Perhaps even more significant was Marimon's crashing into Alberto's Ferrari. While the two of them walked the rest of the way to the Finish, Marimon assuming a look of injured innocence, Gigi Villoresi came into the pits, jumped out of his car and began arguing with officials. He suggested that Marimon had caused the whole thing, baulking so that Fangio, his tutor could win. But when the young Argentinian arrived limping, with blood pouring from a cut over his eyes, he stoutly denied that it was his fault, saying that he couldn't have possibly avoided Ascari's revolving Ferrari. Farina passed no comment whatsoever, although Ascari shot Marimon some pretty nasty looks. Gigi was only too happy that Alberto was unharmed.

Despite all this, Alberto was always the first to make amends; for as he stated in a magazine article: "There exists, between racing drivers throughout the world, a strange, sentimental affinity, a sense of solidarity that often people do not understand. This is that the racing driver has two different attitudes vis-à-vis his rivals. During a race, he struggles with animosity and fury, without pity, against his antagonist, and he is ready to risk his life to obtain victory; in everyday life though, he is chivalrous, and sincerely affectionate. Off-track, we become friends again. My toughest adversaries are Fangio, Farina, Gonzalez, Villoresi, Hawthorn - and among the new arrivals - Marimon and Maglioli. Well then! All these whom I fight against during ten months of the year, continuously risking my life at 200 Km/h speeds - they're all my best friends. They know they can count on me in every situation, and for my part, I am assured of their affection and their reliability.

"In particular, Farina, the World Champion in 1950, a driver who always attacks vigorously, and with whom I have been at crossed-swords on innumerable tracks - has always shown me touching magnanimity and consideration."

Thus a dazzling sequence of Grandes Epreuves ended that September with a raging controversy, following a superb

Maserati-Ferrari duel. World Championship Points finally stood at Ascari 34½; Fangio 28; Farina 26.

The following week, Enzo Ferrari withdrew his entries from the non-championship Modena Grand Prix and Maserati, unopposed, took the first three places.

Soon after, news spread that, after five years of Ferrari, Alberto Ascari and Gigi Villoresi were to leave the House of Maranello and drive for another marque. Why they did this was as intriguing as it was fateful.

"The Missing Jewel"

"Ferrari was a man who liked to divide and rule," Gigi recalls. "He did not voluntarily grieve about his racing drivers. Towards the end of 1953, Alberto and I went up to Modena, but not together - separately - without the one knowing that the other was going. . ."

Alberto: "One day I went to see Ferrari at Modena. He said to me, 'Ascari, I would like to anticipate on January 1st, the signature of the contract which expired on April 30 1954. Do you agree to continue racing for me. I desire that you give me an answer soon and, if you accept, that you must sign the contract immediately.

"I really do not know why Ferrari arrived at this extreme measure, I told him 'Listen Ferrari, I have also had very advantageous offers from other manufacturers. If you can wait until April 30, perhaps I'll decide to race for you. But if you force me to make a decision now, standing here before you I must refuse your offer.' He answered that he couldn't wait. So I did not sign. I returned to Milan the same evening with a sad heart.

"We had known one another for so long. There were too many memories, I had made too many sacrifices for the House of Maranello and the collaboration had given me too much satisfaction to be able to close a chapter as passionate and as attractive in my life, without having some regrets, some nostalgia. Ferrari had honored me with his confidence during such long years and entrusted his magnificent cars and engines to me with the anxiety of a father sending forth his son into the great adventure of life. But I felt it absolutely necessary to find, in the interests of my family above all, a more secure solid economic footing."

Mietta explains: "Alberto did not think that Ferrari paid him well enough for his successes; he complained about this. If he won a Grand Prix, half went to Ferrari, and half went to Alberto - 500 thousand lire each. However, at the same time, the cycling champions received 4 million lire for every race they won. A soccer player was paid even more. Even Press Agents, organizing races for the drivers, earned more than Alberto did. He was not paid in relation to the risks he took."

Gigi adds: "In those days, we were not allowed to accept any publicity or sponsorship payments whatsoever. I don't want to admit how little we were paid, because in the light of today's Formula One drivers' pay, people would take us for blockheads."

It was not just that Enzo Ferrari didn't pay him enough. Nor was it that he simply wanted more time to spend at home with Mietta and the children. No, it was the technical, tactical consideration that by mid-1953 the Grand Prix Formula was to be changed in 1954, to admit cars with engines of 2.5 liters, or 750 c.c. if supercharged. Several companies soon became involved with this new Formula challenge.

At Maranello, under instructions from Commendatore Ferrari, Aurelio Lampredi had attempted to develop the 1953 2-liter V-12 engine to 2.5 liters with 240 h.p. at 7,500 r.p.m. - nothing revolutionary. At Maseratis in Modena, under instructions from Commendatore Omer Orsi, Engineer Colombo had been working on the new 250F Maserati - Maseratis, a firm which with its large electrical components interests, was well able to pay for star drivers.

At Alfa-Romeo in Milan, Engineer Orazio Satta was concerning himself with a very original car, designated the T160. Far away, at Unterturkheim, Stuttgart, West Germany, Mercedes-Benz and their pre-War race manager, Alfred Neubauer, had been making intense preparations for a come-back with their W196 car, rumored to be bristling with innovations. Finally, on September 7 or 8, 1953, a decision was made at the Alpine resort of Merano to create a 2.5. liter Lancia Grand Prix car. In the following week, the decision had to be made as to whether to opt for a 6-cylinder or an 8-cylinder car. Opting for a V-8 cylinder, under instructions from Gianni Lancia in Turin, their Chief Engineer, 63 year-old Vittorio Jano set to work. An ironic reflection: Vittorio Jano had designed the Alfa-Romeo P2 car, driven so successfully and then fatally by Antonio Ascari. Now, 30 years later, he was to design another Grand Prix car.

Alberto was too much of a patriot to sign up with Mercedes Benz and anyway, Fangio had signed up with them, while Gonzalez had switched to Ferrari, eager to compete *against* Fangio instead of *with* him. Alfa-Romeo was out with the old superstitious associations of his father's death at Montlhéry.

Alberto recalled: "The evening of December 29, I closed the door of my study to examine the various propositions which had been made to me. I had received several, from both Italian and foreign companies. Selecting the best offers, concrete and serious, I decided to race for an Italian marque. The following day, in the morning, I left for Turin with Gigi Villoresi; destination Lancia.

"Gianni Lancia and I had known one another for many years. Sincerely interested in racing, I often saw him in the pits following our trials and races and every time we met, I would ask him 'Well, then, when will you decide to build a racing car?' To which he always answered, 'As soon as I have a little time!'"

"At Turin that morning, we told Gianni Lancia that we had left Ferrari, Gigi and I were free. If we could be useful, we were at his disposal.

"Lancia replied, 'O.K. Now we'll see what we'll decide to do. But I feel sure that something good will come out of it. I saluted him and returned to Milan...'"

At 17.15 hours on December 30, 1953, Enzo Ferrari issued an official press release from Maranello:

"On the 31st inst. the tenets of existing collaboration with the race-driver Alberto Ascari will be broken. The root cause of this split, Ascari's desire to direct his future efforts towards creating commercial prospects thus guaranteeing a tranquil future for himself and his family. Scuderia Ferrari reluctantly accepts this decision. Although, understanding the logic of his ambitions, which have induced Ascari to abandon the Company which collaborated with him to the extent of two World Championships, Ferrari is aggrieved that they were not able to offer, now and in the the future, what other companies obviously could to the World Champion."

The announcement that Alberto and Gigi had signed up with Lancia for both sport and Formula One, came on January

1. As Corado Milanta has recalled: "Several days later Alberto came to fetch me and we went to Casella to test the 2.5 liter V-6 Lancia prototype. A miracle had occurred. In three months, a Grand Prix car, bristling with innovations had been designed and built by a company which had never built a Grand Prix car before!"

On January 21, 1954, Alberto announced: "I am now able to tell you with a 99% probability that from this year I shall be racing for Lancia. If something happens with the Lancia deal, I shall go with Maserati, whom I left five years ago. After that, if not Maserati, then to a German company, then to an English company. The journalists have said that I will be racing for Maserati in Grand Prix races until the Lancia 2500 is ready. Not so. I will compete at Sebring. I believe that the Lancia 2500 will be ready by June. If so I will be in time to dispute the last seven races for the World Championship. The Dutch or Belgian Grand Prix could see the baptism of this car."

Alberto and Gigi therefore planned to begin the Season in sportscar events, driving the Lancia C24. In this way they were to be joined by a new team-mate, Eugenio Castellotti, a wealthy, daring, 24 year-old gentleman from Lodi, who had made his name in Italian hillclimbs and endurance races.

Alberto Ascari and Eugenio Castellotti, being of a similar temperament, soon made friends - and in the year to come, the World Champion was to teach this young man, twelve years his junior, some valuable lessons in motor-racing, just as Gigi Villoresi had done with him several years before.

The first experience of this three-some in testing the 3.3. liter Lancia sportscar round the Ospedaletti Circuitat San Remo, in early February, were not exactly encouraging. Corado Milanta recalls:

"One evening Gianni Lancia arrived with the very first Lancia Aurelia Biventi "Spider". In the evening, after supper, I, Ascari and Castellotti decided to go from Ospedaletti to San Remo and we left in this car. Ascari drove, Castellotti in the passenger's seat and I was sandwiched in the middle, my legs either side of the gear stick. At a certain moment, I was chatting with Castellotti, when Ascari suddenly slams on his brakes! A black cat had crossed the road. We were unable to persuade him to drive on - indeed, he returned to the hotel on foot!"

Although Alberto set a new record for the circuit at 66 m.p.h., Gigi's brakes failed on him, he nearly ran over a carabiniere and two children, crashed into a wall and ended up with his badly damaged car jutting out over the edge of the road, beneath which, some 30 meters below, was another road!

Two days later, Alberto and Gigi were returning from San Remo to Milan, when on the ice-slippery road betwen Tortona and Voghera, the Lancia skidded off the road and was wrecked, luckily the two drivers were unhurt.

In early March, Gigi, Alberto, Fangio, Piero Taruffi, Castellotti, Manzon, Valenzano and Rubirosa teamed up in pairs as the four-car Lancia D24 entry for the Sebring 12 hour endurance race in Florida, the U.S.A. The Lancias made an impressive start - Taruffi-Manzon's Lancia leading first, then Ascari-Villoresi's overtaking and building up a good lead in the 2nd hour. In the ensuing hours, Taruffi-Manzon retired with engine trouble; Fangio-Castellotti retired with transmission problems; Ascari-Villoresi retired in the 5th hour with various mechanical problems, primarily transmission. Valenzano-Rubirosa's Lancia came 2nd.

While Alberto was absent in Florida, a court case was held against him in Bresica, where he was accused of manslaughter and assault in that terrible accident during the Mille Miglia road race of 1951 some three years before.

From then on, the champion driver had been deprived of third-party insurance, and in 1952 and 1953 had abstained from competing in the Mille Miglia out of consideration for spectators.

Ascari's lawyers, Aldo Farinello of Turin, Avocato Genovesi of Mantua and Avocato Enrico Sbisa of Milan - proposed that the Defendant could not be held responsible for the accident because he had been dazzled by the lights of a car coming out of a side street. Avocato Sbisa referred to the mitigating circumstance that the Mille Miglia had been competed for on a "closed circuit", officially planned by Prefectorial Ordinances and in that respect, Alberto Ascari could not be held guilty by law. The Defendant, in his absence was acquitted accordingly.

On his return to Italy, therefore, Alberto was relieved in to find that he could once again compete in the Mille Miglia. During the month leading up to it, he and Gigi went into practice along some of the roads involved.

But, thirteen days before the race, on a wet, rainy April 20 at 13.30 hours, Gigi and his mechanic, Secondo Paganelli of Longiano were practising in their 6-cylinder Lancia B22 between Rimini and Riccione. They were racing down the Via Flaminia and came up behind a utility van; Gigi was just overtaking it when the van made to turn left into a side-street. To avoid an accident, Villoresi braked suddenly, but because the asphalt was recently wet from rain, the tyres did not grip the road, the Lancia skidded violently to the right and "We left the road at the only point on 10 Kms where there was a 3 meters-deep ditch. Our car went into it and overturned."

Gigi was seriously cut and bruised on his right-hand side right forehead, right cheek, right eyebrow, right eye, right shoulder etc.. he was also in a serious state of shock. Alberto, Dr. Farina, Valenzano and many others visited the 45 year-old driver and although it looked like he would recover, he was definitely out of the Mille Miglia.

Alberto's distaste for the Mille Miglia was only accentuated by this event; he felt that the Lancia D24 simply was not reliable enough for such a race; but he was now under contract to the Turin firm, and to win was his profession. And it was here that Alberto Ascari, Champion of the World, swallowed his pride and asked Clemente Biondetti - how to win the Mille Miglia.

For Biondetti was the maestro of this 10-hour Endurance Race; in 1938, driving an Alfa-Romeo 2900, he had established a record of 135.391 Km/h on the Florence-Milan autostrada, a record which remained unbeaten until 1953 when Giannino Marzotto broke it in a 4.5. liter Ferrari. And Clemente Biondetti had won the Mille Miglia several times. He told Alberto Ascari that he would only win this race by prudence and by sustaining the courage and determination, despite fatigue, to keep his foot *off* accelerator.

On May 1, the morning before the Start, a truck rammed into Alberto as he set out for a final check of the first

THE MAN WITH TWO SHADOWS

kilometers. The weather at the Start was appalling, with heavy rain. Wearing a black leather suit and light blue helmet, he climbed into the 3.3. Lancia D24 - Number 602 and made a good, undramatic start, at 2 minutes past 6 o'clock, southwards from Brescia towards Verona. Piero Taruffi, driving a similar car, made an electric 115 m.p.h. dash to Verona, foot hard down on the accelerator. Dr. Farina also attempted to make a dashing first leg to Verona, but after only a quarter of an hour, at Peschiera, his car spun round violently and hit a tree, behind which spectators huddled, unharmed; the Doctor was badly injured.

From Verona to Rome, the Lancias of Taruffi, Ascari and Castellotti were battling it out; Taruffi distanced himself by 4½ minutes ahead of Ascari, Just after Rome en route to Florence, Taruffi broke down with engine trouble and loss of oil that kept him out of the race for an hour. The battle was then between Alberto in the Lancia and Paolo Marzotto in a Ferrari. When Paolo Marzotto retired, Alberto passed through Florence and began the route towards Bologna.

Then it happened. The mainspring in the Lancia's accelerator broke and Alberto stopped in the pelting rain, with the Appenine Mountains looming up ahead, just wondering what to do. Unknown to him, Vittorio Marzotto in a 2-liter Ferrari and Luigi Musso in a Maserati were coming up behind him.

Using a makeshift rubber band to fix the mainspring, Alberto drove off in the direction of Bologna, just praying that it would hold! During that very tortuous stretch over the Appenine Mountains, although others retired, amazingly that rubber-band held!

From Bologna, another 80 miles and he arrived at Cremona and crossed the stripe beginning a race-within-a-race: Cremona to Mantua to Brescia - the Nuvolari Grand Prix. The legendary Tazio Nuvolari, had died a lingering death the year before and been buried at Mantua Cemetery. En route to victory, as Alberto Ascari drove his Lancia past that Cemetery, he slowed down and was seen to take his hand off the steering wheel and carry it up to his blue helmet in salute. Thereafter he speeded up and after 11 hours, 26 minutes of driving through the rain at an average 86.7 m.p.h., he arrived back at Brescia, victor of the 1954 Mille Miglia - the only Lancia to finish.

Exhausted, he drove along the Viale Rebuffone where a traditionally large crowd greeted him cheering and applauding. Climbing out, "Ciccio" was lifted up onto their shoulders and carried off, whilst Mietta, ready with a garland of flowers, unable to embrace her husband, followed on.

When interviewed, he calmly commented: "Let it be clear that this victory I owe, before everything else, to the advice given me by Biondetti - advice which I have treasured." Biondetti came 4th in the race.

The Mille Miglia was the purest gem missing from his champion's crown - but now he had got it and proved to his critics that he was also a road-racing driver, capable of keeping two tenths of his potential in reserve for the unknown corner or or the unknown obstacle. His only regret was that his friend and tutor, Gigi Villoresi had not been there to share in that joy.

Not to worry, for in late July, Gigi was to make a superb come-back when he won the 45-lap Oporto Grand Prix in Portugal, driving a Lancia D24 at an average 91.91 m.p.h.; Castellotti came 2nd and Alberto retired with steering-gear trouble.

During those summer months of 1954, the Lancia D.50, Vittorio Jano's novel, Grand Prix 2.5-liter prototype progressed slowly but surely.

Mietta Ascari recalls: "Alberto would often say, 'Yes, yes, in a moment, soon, I'll stop racing', but when someone is on the crest of a wave, it's necessary to keep going forward. Whenever I said I didn't like what he was doing, he would reply, 'This is my job', and I would reply, 'Yes, but rather too dangerous a job, so why don't you consider changing it?'

"In the final years, in fact, he had begun to direct his steps towards joining his Uncle, or in other words, returning to "Agencia Ascari - Commissaria Fiat", under our flat in Corso Sempione. I tried to convince him to work with his uncle - because this had originally been Antonio's agency - but Eliza hadn't earned a penny from it since her husband's death.

"The proposition was that Alberto would become partners with his Uncle's son Ezio and they would have done the agency work together. However, when a time came that his Uncle saw Alberto on the point of leaving racing, he changed his tune: 'Perhaps not, Alberto, for I have now looked after this agency for twenty-five years. It is mine and I want to go on with things the way they are. If you want to come and work here, you can be a salesman.' To which Alberto said, 'No, Thank you. I'd prefer to continue racing.' Afterwards his Uncle regretted his offer, because if he'd made Alberto a partner - everyone would have gone to that agency in the hopes of finding Alberto Ascari there.''

Up until July the Italians and Argentinians had continued their Maserati-Ferrari duel in Alberto and Gigi's absence - with Fangio winning both the Argentine and Belgian Grand Prix.

Then in July, the real prospect of a German offensive in the revolutionary, streamlined form of Herr Klaus's silver W196 Mercedes-Benz Grand Prix car, was causing much consternation in Northern Italy. It was a threat to Italian Grand Prix supremacy. Alberto and Gigi were therefore released by Gianni Lancia to drive 250F Maseratis at the French Grand Prix at Rheims where the Mercedes cars were to make their debut in the hands of Fangio and best-driver, Karl Kling.

They might not as well have bothered. Twenty-one cars started. Only six survived. Fangio and Kling ran away from the field, and after some duelling, crossed the line, one-fifth of a second apart, Fangio averaging 115.67 m.p.h. Alberto fluffed his Start, and on lap 2 blew up his engine trying to keep up with the two Mercedes cars. On exactly the same day, back in Italy, Eugenio Castellotti driving a D24 Lancia, won the Bolzano-Mendola 25Km hillclimb.

One week later, Alberto was back at Monza, testing the Lancia D50 prototype when, at the Vialone Curve, he found that the brakes did not work, the car went off the track, ending up on the infield.

Your father (or mother) died young, at a certain age. When you, the admiring son (daughter) get to that age, are you not tempted, just once, to ask yourself whether you will live to be older than your father (mother)?

Mietta, Gigi Villoresi, Gilberto Colombo, and Aurelio Lampredi have all confirmed that Alberto had a superstitious fear of entering into his 37th year because this was the age in which his father, Antonio, had been killed at Montlhéry - and also the age at which St. Antonio of Padua (whose Saint's day was Alberto's birthday) had died.

Having just celebrated his 36th birthday, Alberto was over at Silverstone, England with Gigi Villoresi and Onofre Marimon as part of the 250F Maserati team for the British Grand Prix. They were late getting there, arrived in complete chaos and had to wait for an unofficial practice session in the evening, which did not, of course, count for grid positions. Thus, on the following rainy, windy day, the unlucky, Alberto found himself right at the very back, 9th row of the Starting Grid, in Car Number 31.

Froilan Gonzalez in a Ferrari, led from Start to Finish, with the Mercedes cars finding that road-holding on the bleak-medium speed Northants airfield was not so very good. Alberto also had a tough time. On lap 9, placed only 7th, he came into the pits and mechanics examined the front suspension and steering links of the Maserati. He went off again, driving furiously, endeavoring to make up for a lost lap. Ten laps later, he was in 17th position, and soon after, the Maserati gave a miniature fireworks display when a valve dropped and he coasted to a standstill beyond the pits' bridge. As usual, Gigi's Maserati was flagged in, and Alberto took over. Driving like a scalded cat, doing his fastest at 1 minute 50 seconds. (95.79 m.p.h.), he even overtook Trintignant's Ferrari for 2nd place, when this second Maserati gave up on him with loss of oil pressure. He came back to the pits and asked, "Any more Maseratis?". As there were none, he packed his bag and left with Gigi, before the crowds clogged the roads.

One week later, Castellotti won another hillclimb in the Lancia D24 - the 31 Km Aosta - Grand San Bernardo.

Alberto did not even turn up at the Nürburgring that year, the year in which Onofre Marimon was killed in his Maserati in practice. - a death which seriously affected Gonzalez. Fangio, driving the W196 Mercedes-Benz, with more orthodox, less furturistic bodywork, won the race on the German Circuit. He also won the Swiss Grand Prix at Bremgarten. In short, Alberto had no hope of retaining his World Title and Italian

Grand Prix supremacy had indeed been toppled.

The Italians were determined that the Germans would not beat them on their own soil. Ferrari-Maserati versus Mercedes. The XXVth Gran Premio d'Italia at Monza. Very generously, Enzo Ferrari allowed Alberto to drive a 2.5 liter Ferrari and he put in a practice lap which placed him alongside Fangio's Mercedes and Stirling Moss's Mercedes on the Front Row of a Grid comprising 20 cars.

He made a slow getaway and on lap 3 was in 3rd place, but then on lap 6 - to huge applause from the crowd - he made his attack and went into the lead from Gonzalez, Fangio and Moss. He continued to hold that lead, cheered on by an immensely partisan crowd, deliriously happy that their idol appeared to have regained his old form. After 10 laps, he was 5 seconds in front of Fangio, the latter driving with brakes which were beginning to fail. On lap 22, Fangio overtook Alberto, but then fell back again, to the great relief of the Autodrome crowds who became demented with joy. But their 'Ciccio' was having to work extremely hard to keep that lead from Juan Manuel - and it became a fierce duel.

Next, on lap 41, Gigi Villoresi snatched 2nd place from Fangio and it seemed as if the inseparable duo were to be "back in business". But then on lap 43, Gigi retired. Alberto now began a passing and re-passing duel with Stirling Moss, but one where, on lap 49, Alberto overstrained his engine, suddenly slowed down, coasted into the pits, climbed out of the Ferrari and made a wide, despairing gesture with his hand which could only mean: "No hope. For me, the race is over!"

When Moss's Maserati suffered badly with a split oil tank, and what the Italians had *most* feared, happened: Fangio on the German Mercedes won the Italian Grand Prix. Moss, however, was the moral victor.

One week later, the World's top drivers were in Northern Ireland for the 21st RAC International Tourist Trophy race at the Dunrod Circuit near Belfast. This race saw the debut of the 3.8 Lancia D25 sportscar and the Turin company sent three of these and a D24 to the Irish Circuit.

The Start of the race, Le Mans style, saw Stirling Moss leading drivers in their sprint across the road to their cars, but the Lancia of Ascari and Villoresi was away first. Soon after though, the two Italians slipped back to 4th place, despite their twice breaking the lap Speed Record averaging 91 m.p.h., and covering the Timed Distance at 143 m.p.h. They retired in the closing stages of the race with a broken prop-shaft; Alberto must have had the fright of his life when that transmission came adrift; the prop-shaft tunnel on a Lancia D25 ran parallel with the driver's thigh and a matter of inches below his left elbow. All of a sudden, a considerable length of shaft, complete with coupling and bolts, tore clean through the sheet metal of that tunnel and made its presence known to Alberto about 3 inches from his upper left trouser leg..!

He had retired in the Dutch Grand Prix, the British Grand Prix, the Italian Grand Prix and the Belfast TT. He had not even competed in the Belgian Grand Prix or the German Grand Prix. He had again refused Ernest Ruis' offer to driver a Kurtis-Offenhauser car at Indianapolis. After 8 victories in 1952 and 11 in 1953, such an anti-climax was bound to have a marked effect. Was the Grand Prix circus passing him by?

There was one more major Grand Prix that year and Lancia were determined that two Formula One D50 cars should compete in it. They therefore arranged a Press Conference in Turin on October 14, ten days before the race.

That afternoon, therefore, Alberto was driving up the Milan-Turin Autostrada at about 75 m.p.h. so as to be up at the Conference on time.

"About 2 Kilometers from Rondissone, I was overtaking a huge petrol tanker, with what appeared to be a clear road in front, when a lorry swung out of a side road, completely blocking my path.

"I had to think quicker than I have ever thought in my life.. .I couldn't swerve off the road because I was hemmed between two walls. I jammed on my brakes. . . the lorry rushed towards me like an express train. I just had time to feel my stomach turn over as when you fail from a roof in a dream...then I saw stars."

His chin hit against the steering wheel whilst his head shattered the windscreen. The car was a write-off. But he climbed out, and hitched a lift the rest of the way! After a quick visit to a medical clinic to get his chin stitched and patched,

Alberto Ascari, calm as ever, appeared at the Press Conference, then allowed himself to be photographed sitting at the wheel of the unpainted, new D50 car.

The 8th Spanish Grand Prix was held on October 24 round the Pedralbes circuit, and saw the debut of two Lancia D50 V-8 engined cars, painted maroon-red at the last minute, and driven by Gigi and Alberto. Now he would be able to show them that an Ascari still meant business.

After a most impressive start, he shot into the lead in the Lancia, jostled by Fangio in the Mercedes, lost it on lap 2, regained it on lap 3 and by lap 8 had built up a big lead, establishing the fastest lap of the race, averaging 100.79 m.p.h. But then on lap 9, a moan of dismay went up as he stopped with clutch problems. He re-started in 14th place, but then came in again, after a very slow lap, and retired. Gigi, driving the other Lancia, ran out of brakes and broke his axle on lap 4 using the gears to stop. The race was won by Mike Hawthorn on a Ferari, but Fangio claimed his second World Championship title in 1954, thanks to the Mercedes Benz W196 and due to the belated arrival of the Lancia D50.

Fangio was not content: "My friend Alberto is a great driver, undoubtedly the strongest that I have ever seen in my racing career. A tip-top man, courageous, calculating and combative, he is extremely hard to beat. Loyal in racing as in his private life; for Ascari I have infinite respect. For this, I would have wanted him for an adversary this year in all the races and not only at Monza. Without him, my victory loses a little of its value. I understand this perfectly and I admit it. This is why I am only half content."

Alberto's chapter of breakdowns and accidents in 1954 came to an end just two days before Christmas. He was practicing in Verona Province for the 1955 Mille Miglia in a Lancia. Arriving at some cross-roads in Valdagno, a motorcyclist suddenly cut across his path. With a lightning maneuver, Alberto swerved to avoid the motorcyclist, just grazing past him and knocking him over. Unharmed the motorcyclist got up, went to remonstrate, recognized the former World Champion and asked him for his autograph! Smiling, Alberto gave him this, then after a little chat, they parted as friends.

"Leap Years Accepted"

"At the beginning of each season, a mad impatience takes hold of my entire being and embraces it - to again find myself on the track, pushing my car to 200 Kilometers an hour in a battle of honor with my adversaries. And, as always, the only vow that I make is 'Il Cielo mi aiuta e che la Fortuna mi sorride!' - may the Sky help me and Fortune smile on me!"

Alberto Ascari: Two World Championships 1952 and 1953; Juan Manuel Fangio: Two World Championships 1951 and 1954. Who would get the Hat-Trick first?

The Argentine Grand Prix on the Buenos Aires Autodrome saw a big turn-out on January 16, 1955. Four Mercedes W196 versus three Lancia D50's versus four Ferraris and six Maseratis. The Lancia team: Ascari, Villoresi and Castellotti - all retired. Fangio (Mercedes), Gonzalez (Ferrari) and Ascari (Lancia) continued to swap for 1st place until lap 31, when Alberto spun off and crashed into a fence.

The Turin team returned home to think again. Just over two months later, the Formula One Lancia clinched its first win, at the home town, in Valentino Park. Again, the Lancias faced 3 Ferraris and 4 Maseratis round the 2.6 mile winding circuit, dear to every Piedmontese.

It was on lap 30, that Alberto, racing Number 6, attacked with all his old mastery and drew away to win by a good margin, averaging 87.83 m.p.h. Villoresi came in 3rd and Castellotti 4th. Vittorio Jano's promising masterpiece, the D.50, with its lateral fuel tanks, would seem to have arrived.

One fortnight later, those Lancias were taken to Pau, nestling under the French side of the Pyrénées. Never in the 16 year-old history of the Pau Grand Prix had the race been won more than twice by the same driver. So could Alberto break that jinx? In practice, he spared the Lancia, Then at the Start, he literally jumped into the lead. But by the first corner, Frenchman, Jean Behra in a Maserati had overtaken him for a few seconds. Now followed an Ascari-Behra duel, with Alberto maintaining his lead all the time, gradually increasing it to the point where by lap 80, he was 40 seconds ahead of the Frenchman.

Misfortune decided to strike on lap 90, with only 20 laps to go. Alberto pulled into his pit with a broken hydraulic brake-line on one of the rear brakes... One by one, they passed him: Behra (Maserati) Castellotti (Lancia), Mieres (Maserati) and Gigi Villoresi (Lancia). Great drivers simply don't give up. Pau 1955 showed Ascari's inborn ability to keep going at all costs. For, two laps later, he went back into that race and completed the remaining laps with only three brakes.

One month later, Alberto Ascari scored the final victory of his life. In front of an excited Southern Italian crowd, on 8th May, he drove the 2.5 liter Lancia D.50 at an average 68,88 m.p.h. round 60 laps of the Posillipo Circuit to win the XIIth Naples Grand Prix. He led from Start to Finish, increasing his average speed with each lap. At the end, the 'tifosi' (fans) lifted him onto their shoulders cheering and applauding because for them, 'Ciccio' Ascari had made that comeback they so badly desired.

A few days later, Alberto turned up in the Lancia D.50 to race in the European Grand Prix at Monaco. The day before the race, in practice, he had succeeded in achieving the fastest lap time, alongside Fangio in the Mercedes - 1' 51"1.

That evening before the race, a group of the drivers, including Fangio and Alberto, went to the cinema, then they went for a stroll around the circuit. When they got to the chicane, the Quai des Etats Unis, that went past the harbor, one of those drivers said, "Whoever touches here, goes into the water". Alberto immediately went and touched something wooden with his hand.

The following day, wearing as usual his blue helmet and blue open-necked shirt, Alberto turned up on the Front Line of the Starting Grid, flanked on either side by Stirling Moss and Fangio in the works Mercedes. Fangio's number was 2 and Moss's 6 Alberto's Number was a combination of those numbers -*26*. Was not this deliberately tempting Fate?

When Antonio Ascari was killed at Monthléry, France on July 26 1925, he was - allowing for nine leap years - 13,463 days to be precise. Whether his ultra-precise son knew it or not, on the 22nd May, Monaco Grand Prix race day, Alberto had lived for 13,462 days. The day after the race, he would be exactly the same age as his father. At this point a student of psychology might well ask 'Subconsciously, did Alberto Ascari feel guilty about wishing to outlive his father?'

It is conceivable that Alberto Ascari asked race organizers to give the Lancia team block numbers 26, 28 and 30, making sure that he got Number 26. In cabalistic Numerology, 8 is a crucial number - and has been so since the ancient Chaldeans. 26 (2 + 6 = 8). Antonio Ascari's P2 Alfa Romeo bore the number on that fateful day at Montlhéry. Alberto had won at Nürburgring in 1951, racing Number 71 (7 + 1 = 8) and the 1954 Mille Miglia, racing Number 602 (6 + 2 = 8). Twice at Spa Francorchamps and also at the 1953 Italian Grand Prix he had raced with the Number 4, (2 x 4 = 8). So, even if he could have arranged that his number at Monaco be 26 - the probability of Fangio's 2 and Moss's 6 either side was coincidence! Stirling Moss recently recalled: "I was not aware of the extraordinary coincidence of Alberto's Racing Number 26, whilst Fangio and I were racing 2 and 6. My favorite number was 7, so if I had had the choice at Monte Carlo I would not have chosen 6, but 7."

The race began, leading up the hill, Fangio was passed by Castellotti's Lancia which then fell back to 2nd, and was then passed by Moss's Mercedes. By lap 10, Fangio led Moss by 10 seconds, who in turn led Ascari, Castellotti and Behra by seven seconds. Ascari and Castellotti took it in turns to pass and re-pass each other. Before long, the two Mercedes were running in close company and apparently unassailable. On lap 50, Fangio retired with transmission trouble, and Moss went into the lead and began to lap all the went into the lead and began to lap all the other competitors, some more than once. By lap 80, Moss had got to the point where before long, he would even lap Alberto's Lancia, still in 2nd place and 90 seconds behind.

But this was not to be, for he completed the next lap in a cloud of smoke as oil spewed onto hot exhausts from his broken engine and the Englishman was forced to retire. But Alberto did not know this. He roared out of the dark tunnel under the Casino and back into the blinding sunshine in pursuit of a non-existent leader. Little knowing that he himself was leading, could slow down a little and stood to win the first event in the 1955 World Championship Series.

Neither was this to be. The Lancia rushed down the ramp to the chicane, a barricaded jog that carried the race onto the quay bordering the Bay of Hercules, the Quai des Etats Unis, overlooking the luxury yachts and motor cruisers decked with fluttering pennants. Either due to a brake too tired to function after 800 corners, or to a fractured steering drop arm touching the ground, the Lancia went out of control at 100 m.p.h., hit the kerb, skidded back over a slick of oil left by Moss's ailing Mercedes, crashed through a wooden palisade and straw bales, passed miraculously between two cast iron mooring bitts, somersaulted some 50 yards through the air and then plummeted into the harbor in a geyser of spray and steam that towered like a depth charge. He had hit the palisade at the precise point where he had 'touched wood' the evening before.

For a dreadful twenty seconds, the swirling green surface gave only a few oily bubbles, while divers prepared for just this emergency, scrambled into action. A pack of cars roared by, the last slowing as its driver twisted in his seat looking back. It was, of course, Gigi Villoresi, his friend. Then people were shouting - "There he is!" - as a blue helmet bobbed to the surface, and Ascari's streaked face was seen beneath it. Alberto tore off the helmet, but still holding it, he struck out with a strong over-arm, until divers had reached him and pulled him aboard their rescue boat.

To have missed those cast-iron mooring bitts by inches and not to have been knocked unconscious or caught in the sinking car was a bonus of luck. . .

While Alberto was taken to hospital with slight forehead injuries, painful nose, a damaged right thigh, bruises all over and considerable shock, Maurice Trintignant, driving a Ferrari, won that European Grand Prix. Alberto's $90,000 Lancia was located in 8 meters of water that Sunday evening. As a crane hauled its mangled wreckage up out of the water, it was observed in the floodlights that its wheels had been almost torn away from the rest of the chassis. It was immediately loaded onto a trailer, which went off in the direction of Turin.

The following day, Alberto, in Monte Carlo Hospital, played it ultra calm, eating an ice-cream and telling people it was, "Nothing, nothing. All in a day's work. Fortunately I can swim and know how to breathe underwater."

Although doctors suspected a damaged spine and damaged nose, and suggested he stay on at the hospital to recover better, Alberto insisted he "felt fine." It was May 23 and he was exactly the same age as his father - to the day.

On May 24, as Mietta remembers: "Gianni Lancia sent us a chauffeur-driven car to take us back to Milan. En route, we went to see a site on the Riviera where a friend of ours planned to build holiday villas - and then back home. On our arrival at Corso Sempione, we were very amused to find that the Italian Motornautical Federation had presented him with a life-jacket for future races - just in case!"

May 25: After check-up with his doctor, Alberto met up with his friend Gilberto Colombo, who recalls: "Describing his accident, he told me, 'It was so strange, I was driving through Monte Carlo, and I suddenly found myself taking a bathe in the harbor!' That day we had to go to Lancia, because he had to take his every day car for a small repair job. So he said to me, 'Look, Gilberto do me a favor. You drive, because this leg is annoying me a little.' So I drove his Lancia and we later returned home to his flat.

" 'D'you know something? They're doing trials up at Monza for the sportscar race this Sunday,' he said.

" 'What does that mean Alberto,' I asked, 'that we're going up there tomorrow, or that we're not going?' Then I added, 'Look Alberto, why bother? There's no reason for you to go up there!'

" 'Perhaps not. Look, I know what we'll do Gilberto,' he said. 'I'll get up around 11 o'clock and I'll telephone you. Because if we see that there's no need to go up to Monza, we'll make an appointment together to go out and eat 'un bel risotto alla Milanese!' Those were the last words my friend, Alberto Ascari, ever spoke to me."

The IIIrd Supercortemaggiore 1000 Km race for sportscars was scheduled to take place at the Autodrome on the following Sunday. Before the Monaco race, Alberto had arranged to co-drive in this race with Eugenio Castellotti in the latter's new, 3-liter Ferrari sportscar; Láncia had given them permission to do this.

Immediately after his arrival back from Monaco, Castellotti had gone straight up to the Autodrome to put his still un-painted car through its trials.

Mietta recalls the morning of May 26: "Alberto was always one who, if he could, liked to 'lie-in' on the morning, sometimes until midday. At 10 o'clock that morning, when Castellotti phoned our flat, Alberto was sleeping. Speaking from his bed, I heard him say, 'Yes, alright, I'll come up. I'll probably arrive before midday.' Alberto then told me that Castellotti had invited him to watch some trials up at Monza. He got up calmly, had breakfast, did his toilette and just before he left, told me, 'I'll be back home by one o'clock, so you can make some lunch.'"

When Alberto arrived around 11.30, Castellotti had completed a further 25 laps at 112 m.p.h. But Gigi, who was already there, at once told Alberto that the Ferrari's speed was still inferior to that of the 3-liter Maserati sportscar that he, Gigi, was going to drive on Sunday. For the first time in seven years, instead of also racing the same marque of car, Gigi, "for old times sake" had chosen a Maserati. In short, Gigi and Alberto had become rivals; "Guerrino Bertocchi had said there was another Maserati sportscar at Alberto's disposal should he want it - but Alberto preferred to race a car from Maranello."

Together with Gigi, Eugenio, Count Gianni Lurani, Sportorno, Restelli and three Ferrari mechanics, Bazzi, Nava and Meazza, Alberto went to the Grandstand Restaurant. Chatting with his admiring circle of friends, Alberto recalled his ducking in the Bay of Hercules, told them laughingly about his new lifejacket. Although when asked, he complained of a slight numbness in his thigh, a stiffish back and a strange feeling inside his nose, Alberto, as usual played down his grievances. Also present was Cenzo Monte, the Mayor of Vimercate, a friend of Castellotti, who had brought with him a salami sausage which he shared out. Alberto agreed to eat a breadroll and drink a cup of tea. Despite all this, those that knew him, observed that something, they knew not what, was making him a little tense.

Was it the date-day - the 26th of the month? Was it even, as mentioned before, that he knew that while his father Antonio had lived 13,463 days, he Alberto having so far lived 13,466 days, had lived for just three days longer than his father?

Between 1200 and 1300 hours, they left the restaurant and went across to the Ferrari. Gigi decided not to follow them, simply because he did not want Alberto or Eugenio or the others to think that he was involving himself in matters that did not concern him.

As they walked towards the Ferrari, Alberto quietly told Lurani, "You, Gianni, also know that after a crash it is better to put yourself back behind the steering wheel as soon as possible."

Castellotti was about to climb back into his Ferrari for further trials when, out of the blue, Alberto asked, "Eugenio, d'you mind if I climb into the cockpit - just to see whether my back is not too stiff?"

Having taken off his jacket, he slowly and painfully eased himself into the driver's seat. Once sitting there, came a further request: "I'd like to try her out - just to see if I'm OK for Sunday. I'll only make three or four laps. I'll drive slowly!"

As neither Bazzi nor Meazza had any objection to this, Castellotti readily consented.

As mentioned before, Alberto Ascari would never drive without either his talisman blue helmet or his blue-open-necked shirt. But that famous helmet was at present having a new chin strap fitted after the Monte Carlo incident. So Alberto borrowed Castellotti's white helmet, which was a little too small for him, then his gloves and his goggles. Nor did he bother to take off his tie, knotted around a blue silk shirt. Watching from a distance, Gigi was absolutely astonished.

Completing the first, slow lap around an Autodrome which was about to be rebuilt, restoring two giant, banked curves to the glory they had enjoyed in Antonio's day - an Autodrome with which he had been familiar since as a little child he had

seen his father race to victory - Alberto was clocked at 2' 57"
(95.81 m.p.h.) Then the second lap was a little faster - 2' 9"
(109.19 m.p.h.) As he passed the judges stand, he waved "I'm
OK" - just as he had done once at the Indianapolis Speedway,
three years before. . . As he put his foot down to see what the
Ferrari was like at higher speeds, those at the Autodrome knew
that the maestro was getting back into his stride. Through the
Lesmo double-bend for the 9th time in his racing career, and
onto the straight which led into the great, familiar left-hand
curve of Vialone, a curve that is so gradual that it is hardly a
curve at all, and was normally taken at high speed by "Ciccio"
with no trouble at all.

Those waiting for him to complete that lap heard repeated
changes of gear, then seconds later, the engine roar suddenly
stopped. There was an ominous "clank-clank-clank". Then
silence. Then a man came running up the track, waving his
arms and looking terribly distressed.

Gigi Villoresi lifted his hands to his face in utter despair.
Several of them ran excitedly up the straight in front of the
Grandstand that finishes on the Porfido Curve. The sight that
met their eyes was ghastly. Alberto was lying in a pool of blood,
unconscious - and further on lay the car, mangled and upside
down.

"Aftermath"

Standing not far from the Vialone Curve was Valdo Crippa, another Autodrome worker, who later reported as follows: "I suddenly saw the car swerve outwards, almost to the point of hitting the straw bales. The driver was desperately trying to put her back on course and it seemed as if he had done so. Suddenly, however, the car pointed itself in the opposite direction, towards the inside of the curve, leaning over frighteningly on its right side. Then, as if its nose had dug into the soil, the car lifted itself up vertically some several meters, then bounced back onto the ground, grazing it, then made a second jump (in which moment Ascari was thrown out of the cockpit) and finally went and fell onto the edge of the asphalt border. The upturned vehicle continued along the ground for some ten meters."

Alberto lay on his back on the soil, unconcious. He was ten meters away from the car; Castellotti's white helmet, smashed into two jagged pieces, was a little way away from him; one shoe was lying on the track and the other near the car. Alberto's face was covered with blood and there was a fearful hole in his forehead, just to the right. They undid his tie, and felt his pulse. It was beating very faintly. The ambulance soon arrived. His mechanic immediately offered a blood transfusion. They lifted him onto the stretcher and up into the ambulance, Gigi climbing aboard to be with his friend.

En route to Monza Hospital, Alberto Ascari gave a shudder and died in Gigi's arms...

Post-mortem later revealed that he had died of multiple injuries, including a smashed skull, a fractured jaw, completely fractured left shoulder, completely fractured pelvis and so on. He had virtually been crushed to death.

Sobbing, Gigi telephoned his sister, Rosy Villoresi who, with a mutual friend of the two champions, went to Corso Sempione 60 to give the news to Mietta whom Alberto had phoned just before making those trial laps. She was expecting Alberto's customary telephone call to say that "everything is fine". One simply could not tell her - or her mother-in-law, Signora Eliza, such tragic, traumatic news on a telephone...

"I'll tell you a strange thing. Through all those nine years, as his wife, you live in terror of something happening to him, of his being killed. But that midday, eating and chatting with the children, I felt no terrible premonitions. It was neither a race day, nor a day of practice. He had only gone up there to watch the trials - not to drive. Therefore I was calm,. Then this friend, arrived, the husband of Mila Shun, a famous Milan dressmaker and told me that Alberto had been involved in a bad accident at Monza, and that I had best go up there with him. But I couldn't believe it."

Towards 13.30, another telephone rang in the office of Scuderia Lancia in Corso Vittorio, Turin. Attilio Pasquarelli, the sporting director of the Turin team lifted the receiver "Pronto!", on the other end of the line, the voice of Castellotti, broken by sobs, gave the terrible news. Pasquarelli turned pale as a sheet and did not make a sound for several seconds. He then made the young driver repeat what he had said, word for word, for he did not believe him. Putting down the telephone, Pasquarelli put his head between his hands with a great cry. In the next room was Gianni Lancia. Pasquarelli got up like an automaton, opened the door and repeated the words with a trembling voice;

"Alberto is dead".

Lancia called Vittorio Jano, who in 1925 had seen the death of Antonio Ascari at Montlhéry. The three of them left Turin for Monza within the hour.

Soon after, Mietta arrived at Monza Hospital and entered the mortuary. When she saw her husband's battered corpse, she broke down into an hysterical fit of sobbing.

Ironically, Aurelio Lampredi, who had been present at so many of Alberto's victories and defeats was not up at the track that day: "After returning from Monte Carlo, I was dead tired, having passed three long days getting the cars in order for the Grand Prix. So, while getting the Ferrari sportscars sent over to Monza for Supercortemaggiore with our mechanics, I went home to Modena, telling them, 'If there's something wrong, give me a ring. I am tired, I'm going home. I'm no good to anyone.'

"Thursday at midday they telephoned me, telling me that there had been an accident and that Alberto Ascari had been killed. I did not even have the strength to say 'What happened?', but put down that telephone, went to my car and drove off. I don't know where I went. I drove around for half a day like a lunatic and returned that evening without knowing where I had gone. . ."

That afternoon, somewhat morbidly, several hundred people converged on the Autodrome and on the Vialone Curve to see the remains of the crash - including photographers, film and TV cameramen, and experts. In contrast a more pious person placed a bunch of red gladioli over the place where he had lain.

The evidence was there alright. At the exit to that curve the Ferrari would seem to have swerved to the left; its side-slip was marked out by four graze-marks, of which two were more marked and branched off, some 50-60 meters. At this point the car was skidding further and further sideways, the distance between the two extremities of the traces corresponding to the wheelbase of the Ferrari 3-liter sportscar - 2.20 meters. Signs of the struggle, of the skidding of the car's wheels escaping the driver's control. Then suddenly those black lines stopped - re-appearing 15-20 meters later - while the projectile flew through the air, throwing out the driver. In fact, whilst the tell-tale signs of a skidding car were missing, instead, running along the asphalt - in stretches - three traces very close together, and parallel. Starting from the center of the track, the first trace was blue and formed by little shreds of the driver's shirt; the second was bloody; the third, yellow in color, came from the cork of the white helmet.

Following this, a furrow re-appeared on the asphalt, possibly left by the broadside movement of the abandoned car as it went off the track broadside; then further on again, another furrow showing its landing after that first jump; finally, gone berserk, the car had opened up a pathway, razing a swathe of shrubs and bushes, a broad slice of vegetation - before it stopped, upside down, at least 250 meters from the initial black skid marks.

As for the car itself, it had soon been righted. It was crumpled like paper in its bodywork. The wood-rimmed steering wheel was splintered and contorted. The rev counter read 6000 revs.

and the gear lever was in fifth gear - which, when combined suggested that when he left the track, the driver had been doing between 110 and 125 m.p.h. The Ferrari 3000 Sport was capable of hitting speed around 145-150 m.p.h. But all in all, Ferrari mechanics and experts found nothing wrong with the car.

For a few minutes that afternoon, the workers of the Lancia factory in Turin, the Maserati factory at Modena and the Ferrari factory at Maranello stopped work in homage to the great champion. Late that afternoon the children, Tonino and Patrizia, were rushed away to a country villa belonging to Gianni Lancia. There they stayed for several days, looked after by a maid who had stopped the post so that it would not bring the newspapers and had taken the valves out of the radio so that no broadcast should be heard. . .

That night, Ascari's body lay in state at Monza Hospital Chapel, where he had been given Absolution. It was dressed in blue, draped with the Italian Tricolor, the hands were still covered with his racing racing gloves, and there was a zinc-framed glass coffin lid overall so mourners could look down for the last time at their idol and hero. Hundreds filed past his body. Among them, a tear-stained Enzo Ferrari, who stood in front of the heavily-carved coffin and remembered the little boy of thirty years before.

Flower wreaths and telegrams came from all over the world, including one from General Peron, and another from an absolutely stunned and unnerved Juan Manuel Fangio ("I never thought that Ascari could be a victim of a serious accident. I admired his incontestable qualities as a driver and his assurance in every situation. We were great friends and the news of the death of my friend has been an extremely painful shock.")

The tough, Nino Farina, heard the news late the night on his car radio, while travelling to the Nürburgring. "The knowledge of another accident to him so soon after the first one - and which carried him away so suddenly, prevented me from continuing the journey. I became so disturbed that I had to hand over the steering wheel to my companion."

At 2 o'clock on May 27, the zinc coffin was replaced with a wooden one, a wreath of red carnations and white roses, with the words ("From Your Mietta and your children, Tonino and

Patrizia") was placed on top; and on top of that, the legendary blue helmet. At 3.30, escorted by a police motorcycle escort, the hearse bearing that coffin arrived in Milan. Throughout the journey into his home city, a vast and silent crowd - comprising thousands of motor-racing fans and many who had never seen a race - paid homage and had literally thronged the square in front of the church of San Carlo al Corso. From the front columns of this Church, hung black drapes and a big inscription: "On the Last Finish Line, meet, O Lord, the soul of Alberto Ascari." Following the ornamental hearse, numerous cars bearing the ever-growing flower-wreath tributes - inside and out. The middle-aged and elderly citizens of Milan, those who could remember, were reminded of Antonio Ascari's final homecoming, some thirty years before.

The coffin was carried into the church by the drivers of the 'Scuderia Ambrosiana', of whom Alberto had been one: Villoresi, Castellotti, Carlo and Massimo Leto di Priolo, Nicosia and Spotorno.

The funeral took place on the following morning - Saturday May 28. There had never been anything quite like it since the War. Again, Milan came out in its thousands to mourn and watch the funeral procession. The wreaths, bearing flowers of every description, filled ten cars. As the cortege slowly wound its way through the city, people threw more flowers out of their windows and onto the hearse below, as it passed by. when the procession arrived along Corso Sempione, it came to a halt in front of the Ascari's house, No.60.

Out onto the 2nd floor balcony, stepped Signora Eliza Marelli, the long-time widow of Antonio Ascari and the mother of the dead driver whom a long time ago, she had in vain tried to stop following in his father's footsteps. The old lady, supported by Dr. Giuseppe Farina's wife, looked down in sad dignity at the hearse. To pay her last respects to her son, she made a sign with her hand through the air, then returned indoors. The cortege moved on, finally coming to the Monumental Cemetery and the family tomb. As the last rites were pronounced, Gigi Villoresi, himself demented with grief, bravely supported Mietta, who was unable to stop crying.

Among the countless eulogies written to Alberto Ascari,

perhaps that of Giovanni Canestrini in "Gazzetta Sportiva", is most worth documenting. Canestrini, arguably the greatest and most seasoned motoring journalist Italy has ever produced was an extremely close friend of Alberto's and followed his career from start to finish: "I never called him 'Ciccio' - it pleased neither him nor me - especially to call a World Champion, representing our country by such a name - a pet-name so popular, which among other things contrasted strongly with his character and his style.

"I don't know who might have begun to call me by this name; certainly not my family. It must have been Brera who had a passion for giving everyone nicknames. . . But Gigi always called him Alberto.

"Alberto Ascari was above all a good-natured man; adaptable, and seemed a maleable character, ready to compromise, disposed towards passing over his own ideas and welcoming those of others through love of a quiet life; -lacking pride and will. He was indeed the opposite. His secret was clear cordiality, that apparently meek manner of his, that communicative, distinctly Ambrosian approach and that affability which would seem to renounce real ideas, but was in reality, only superficial and formal.

"Alberto Ascari knew what he wanted and did what he wanted to do; and succeeded without predisposed attitudes, without hurting anyone's feelings, and without exaggerating his wishes.

"He was fully aware of his power and value as a driver, but above all of his responsibilities and his duties as 'champion'. He had a rigorous respect for his profession and for the strictest of mental discipline. He was apparently an optimist, but deep down was above all, a realist, who was consistent and faced the problems of life and of racing, very practically and without academic or sentimental diversions.

"I feel that Alberto Ascari had not yet totally fulfilled either his potential or desires, and that his career was tragically interrupted just while he was in reach of its zenith. He had his own personality, well defined, distinct; his style recalled that of Bordino, but was more vehement, even more brilliant, more decisive; he had a concept of a race, of combat, which was unique, similar to Nuvolari but even more contained, more reasoned, less instinctive; he had the acuteness, the emotional self-control, the meticulousness of Varzi, but through his expansive and apparently meek character, these gifts were less obvious. He had the optimism, the style of driving, the exuberance of Rosemeyer and of Caracciola he possessed the power, the tenacity, the seriousness.

"If he had been able to arrive at his maturity, he would certainly have been the most complete driver who had ever existed; perhaps it is equally so that the technical results reached by him, show themselves without a doubt to be equal to those of the greatest drivers of the past.

"We have lost him while he was entering the culminating phase of his art and of his style - and it seems we have lost everything. . ."

Three days after the funeral, Lancia officially suspended all racing activity - but Castellotti decided otherwise, that the best way to pay tribute to Alberto's memory was not to withdraw, but to compete in the Lancia D.50 and try to win. On June 4, whilst in Buenos Aires, Argentine race drivers and fans were attending a special mass in memory of Alberto Ascari, Eugenio Castellotti, on his own, was racing a "private entry" Lancia D.50 in the Belgian Grand Prix at Spa-Francorchamps. But Fangio, who led all the way, averaging 118 m.p.h. made the fastest road race ever run in Europe.

By the end of July 1955, a public fund of some $34,000 had been raised to go towards Mietta and the children - another tribute to Alberto's popularity. Also in July, Lancia, in financial trouble, handed over six Lancia D.50 cars, engines, blueprints and spares over to Ferrari; with them went Eugenio Castellotti.

On the freezing and foggy morning of December 6, a marble plaque slab was unveiled at the Valentino Park in Turin, to commemorate Alberto's last race on this circuit. It read:

6

ALBERTO ASCARI

1955

Present at the ceremony were Mietta, Castellotti, Valenzano and Dr. and Mrs. Farina - not to mention representatives from Maserati, Ferrari, Lancia, Pirelli etc.. Later, at the monumental Cemetery, a bronze bust of Alberto was unveiled alongside the existing bronze bust of Antonio. Later again, the fatal Vialone Curve at Monza was re-named Ascari Curve. Thus there are now two Ascari Curves - one at Montlhéry and one at Monza.

And as for the others? In the same season Fangio by winning the remaining Dutch, Swedish and Spanish Grand Prix, Fangio clinched his third World Championship for Mercedes. When Mercedes retired at the end of the year, the Argentinian switched to Ferrari and won the 1956 World Championship then he switched again to win his fifth World Championship with Maserati in 1957. His last race was the 1958 French Grand Prix, and thereafter he retired on his laurels, arguably the greatest racing driver of all time. Had Alberto lived, Juan Manuel's task might have been considerably tougher.

By 1957, Eugenio Castellotti had already begun the climb to the summit of his career - as the pupil and successor to Ascari. he had won the 1956 Mille Miglia and also come 1st Overall with Fangio in the Sebring Twelve Hours in Florida. His duels with Luigi Musso for the Italian Championship title bordering on the reckless, had fired the Italian public. And he had fallen desperately in love with Delia Scala, a beautiful "soubrette" actress.

In fact, in mid-March 1957, Castellotti was in Florence with Delia Scala, on holiday, when he received a telephone call from Enzo Ferrari at Modena. Jean Behra, driving a Maserati, had set up some extremely threatening lap times for the Modena Autodrome. The track record for Modena Autodrome had always been held by Ferrari. It was a question of pride. Ferrari required Castellotti up at Modena to defend the honor of Maranello the 2.5 liter Lancia-Ferrari V8 car.

Out of condition, a tired Castellotti arrived at Modena on March 14th, having left Florence at 5 o'clock in the morning. He climbed into the Lancia-Ferrari, made several warming-up laps, and then made a sign to the pits that he was going to go faster. He was approaching the South-West S-variant of the Autodrome, when his car went berserk at over 100 m.p.h. and crashed into a concrete wall, 10 centimeters thick. Some say it was a dog crossing the track, others that the accelerator pedal mechanism was faulty. 27 years-old, Eugenio Castellotti died on the way to hospital of head wounds and multiple injuries.

Gigi Villoresi recalls: "It was concerning Castellotti's death that my friendship with Ferrari was broken. For the sake of Ferrari's pride, challenged that day over a cup of coffee in the Biella Club at Modena, was it right to have put in jeopardy the life of a racing driver?"

The following year, another hopeful, Luigi Musso, was killed on July 7th in the French Grand Prix at Rheims.

Dr. Nino Farina also had an ironic demise. In May 1956, during trials for the IVth Supercortemaggiore sportscar race at Monza, the Doctor's Maserati crashed at over 100 m.p.h., hurtled into a straw bale, somersaulted and he was pinned under the 2-liter car; he suffered two broken ribs, a broken collarbone, and face cuts - but survived. In 1957, he spent 25 million lire on an American-built car, complete with mechanic, for the Indianapolis 500 race - only to have his stand-in driver, Andrews, crash it in practice: Andrews was killed and the car was a write-off.

In October 1960, Farina decided to go and play golf; leaving his car behind, he went in his friend's 1100. One hour later the car crashed against the parapet of a bridge; Farina was seriously injured, but his friend was killed instantly. Although the Doctor swore he was not driving, witnesses said he was; The Ivrea Court found him guilty and he was duly sentenced. Even though Farina swore by his Madonna della Conciliata, the Press attacked him and no-one would believe him. It was the end of a legend.

One day, an old friend from Geneva called George Filippinetti appeared, offering him a new job with his son Jean Pierre. Farina regained his former optimism at the prospect. But one summer's day in 1966, the 60 year-old Doctor climbed into his white Lotus Cortina and, as usual, made for Geneva. In the neighborhood of Chambery, on a road which, although he knew it perfectly well, was wet and slippery, Farina skidded on an angular curve and crashed, with fatal injuries to the former Grand Prix Champion. Some said he must have fallen asleep at the wheel, for why else should such a man, who had battled his way through such a dangerous sport, die in such a banal way? Soon after, Mrs. Else Farina suddenly discovered that she had become an extremely wealthy woman; her husband, who had once described his only *other* ambition was "to become a businessman in the field of finance", had for years been secretly leaving all his money in a Swiss Bank!

Gigi Villoresi has been more fortunate. Fifteen months after Alberto's death, Gigi raced for the Rome Grand Prix round the Castelfusano Circuit, in the middle of pine forest, almost by the sea: " I was lapping another competitor, who had signalled me to pass him. I had placed myself for the corner when he changed his position. I was forced to put my wheels into the sand, the car went out of control and crashed against a large pine tree. I was catapulted out of the car. They found me unconscious with all my left side smashed-in and bleeding seriously. They operated on me for three hours in a Rome hospital, and flew me back to Milan on a special flight. At the beginning of 1957, I decided to retire from motor-racing and devote my time to my car agency, selling Innocenti Mini-Motors."

In January 1960, the team of Villoresi and Capelli were seen driving a Fiat 1500 in the Monte Carlo Rally. But then their car skidded in the snow and hit a stationary motor lorry in the neighborhood of Sid, between Belgrade and Zagreb. Gigi was slightly injured and they retired.

Today, Gigi Villoresi is 71 years-old and lives in Milan. Together, with Piero Taruffi, these two have become the Grand Old Men, who have survived that hecatomb known as Motorsport. In 1955, Aurelio Lampredi left Ferrari for Fiat in Turin, where he has been ever since, the Chief Designer for all the most modern Fiat engines of the last twenty years, (Dino, 124, 125, 127, 128, 130, 132, 1050, Panda etc.) And even today, the man who created "Ferrari Music" in the 1950's still waxes nostalgic about his other boyhood ambition, the one he never fulfilled; to be the conductor of a symphony orchestra!

Finally, Alberto's son, Tonino Ascari:- Although there were toy cars and photographs of his father in his bedroom in Corso Sempione, Tonino had never seen his father race. In 1960, aged 18, Mietta sent him to Coventry, England, where he worked for

Jaguars and learned to speak English. Returning to Milan, he got a job in the Engineering Department of Alfa-Romeo, then another job working in Gigi Villoresi's Innocenti-Mini Agency. Then he became involved with the building of racing cars for the Formula Junior 1,000 C.C. Class, cars made by local constructors such as Stanguellini and Foglietti.

"Starting by watching them being built, I naturally became interested in testing them, and then in racing them."

On August 2 1963, Tonino became 21 years-old and inherited a sum of money. Against his mother's wishes, (his grandmother, Eliza, had died three years before), some 27 days later, on August 29, he drove a Formula Junior car belonging to Angelo Dagrada, round Monza - the track so well known to his father and grandfather. By October he was attending the school course for drivers at the Vallelunga Autodrome near Rome, driving a 2.5. liter Ferrari. One month later, Tonino was up at Modena Autodrome, taking racing lessons in a 2-liter, two-seater Cooper-Maserati sportscar from his father's old rival, Piero Taruffi, whose idea it had been to create a little stable of young pilots - the Scuderia Centro-Sud. Also taking lessons was Farina's nephew.

On April 15 1964, Enzo Vigorelli announced that Tonino Ascari would race for two years with a Foglietti-Olbay Formula Three car under the colors of the Scuderia Madunina. That year, Tonino Ascari became Overall Champion of Italy in Formula 3,, whilst Formula 2 Champion was a promising newcomer called Ernesto Brambilla.

"My participation in motor-racing," Tonino has recalled, "came from my own personal curiosity; that is, I experimented, enjoyed it, was amused by it and it gave me valid sensations. I raced for three years, then left the sport so that I could devote more time to an agency that myself and a friend were building up selling Italian and Japanese motorcycles.

'When I started, the Press at once decided to dub me, "The New Ascari", "The Third Ascari", and to expect big things of me. But you don't suddenly become a champion in only three years. It's necessary to break cars, to win races and to pass from one Class up to the next. And in fact, it is true that I found it hard to exist under the two, strong shadows of my grandfather and father. If I were to succeed, people would say that it was not because I was better than the others, but because I was my father's son. If I were to fail, then the dynasty was finished and the grandson should not have attempted to continue it.

"Then there was something else. Unfortunately I found a sponsor extremely interested in exploiting my name for publicity and other motives. As I did not want my name to be used by someone else for profit, I left the sport, never having accepted sponsorship. Had I had my own money, I would perhaps have continued racing. I also left the anxieties of motor-sport when I realized that they were of relative unimportance."

In mid-May 1978, Tonino was exactly the same age - to the week - as his father Alberto had been when he had been killed some twenty-three years before. "But I did not let my knowledge of this recurrence of dates influence me, because I was no longer a racing driver when I reached that age. I was, and am, a car dealer, with responsibilities to a wife, to two small children and to a mother - and had I thought about such things, I would never had left our house."

In May 1979, the Cambridge Road Garage, British Alfa-Romeo dealers, having long felt the need for a "production" Alfa to compete with the Gordinis, the Golf GTI's and the Talbot TI's, decided that as Alfa-Romeo of Italy had no immediate plans to bring out a Veloce engine TI, that they - Bob Murray and Tim Abady - would modify, custom build and tune up some two-door and four-door 1.5 liter Alfa-Sud road cars. Many hours were spent working on the specification and testing of the prototype, which, when placed on the Rolling Road, indicated 103 bhp at 5500 rpm and a quick acceleration to 108 mph. Their search for a special name made them reject titles like "Super Sports" etc. Then they looked at the names of historic Alfa-Romeo racing drivers. They rejected Campari on the basis that Porsche had used that name. So they called it the CRG Ascari. The first one of these "specials" was delivered in August 1980. So far a dozen CRG Ascaris have been delivered, not to mention conversions done to existing Alfa-Suds. With this book and this car, it would seem that the Ascari name has re-appeared to the public. At the time of going to press, the

Cambridge Road Garage are still building CRG Ascaris to order.

"The Mathematics Of Destiny"

The biggest question mark that remained - and still remains to this day, some twenty-five years later, is as to why Alberto Ascari, one of the finest and luckiest drivers the World has ever seen, came to grief, testing a car at below Grand Prix speeds around an empty track on a clear day, and round a corner that was not a corner at all...

To others, the Vialone Curve was notoriously tricky; other drivers such as Sanesi and Zanardi had left the track at this point. Alberto had once joked, half in earnest to Autodrome officials: "I would feel much happier if you could widen it with a little more asphalt!"

Piero Taruffi, in his autobiography, has commented: "Visiting the scene of the accident shortly afterwards, I examined the tyre marks and noticed a peculiar thing: more than halfway round the corner, that is, when the driver was in sight of the straight and might have been expected to let the car run wide, reducing the cornering forces on it, he had unaccountably *tightened* his turn, heading for the inside verge. It so happens, moreover, that the road here dips slightly - initiating the slide which developed into an uncontrollable spin. How could Alberto, with his great knowledge of racing, knowingly take such a line. . .?"

Recently interviewed, Stirling Moss has suggested: "If you have anywhere, a fairly long gear selection rod and you get any torsional stresses in the chassis, you can get to the point where you get a slight twist, so that instead of the thing pushing it in straight back from 4th to 5th, it went into 3rd. This would have given an instant slight lock on the back axle, and the car would have started to side-skid. If he had been right on the edge of adhesion, a slight lock on the back rather than on the driver would have certainly started to make the car do something. But this is conjecture on my part. I just don't think that Ascari, with his ability, would have lost it on that corner."

Mike Hawthorn had arrived at the Autodrome just one hour after the crash and also co-drove a 3-liter Ferrari with Maglioli in the Supercortemaggiore Race that Sunday. In his auto-biography, "Challenge Me the Race", Hawthorn commented: ". . .or he had missed a gear, changing into 3rd where he should have been getting fifth. I believe the explanation is quite different. The tyres we wanted to use for these cars were 6.50 - 16, but they were not available at the time in the particular make we were using, and so 7.00 - 16 covers had been fitted. I had driven the car with these tyres on it, found it very nasty indeed when it came to the Vialone Curve, where there were a lot of little ripples in the road surface. I came to the conclusion that the rims were too narrow for these tyres and I had them taken off my car. Where Ascari crashed there were long, broad, black tyre marks, followed by marks of the wheel rims digging into the road, and it seemed to me that he probably changed into fifth speed just as he hit the ripples, the car started to slide, and tyres rolled under and the rims gouged into the road, causing it to somersault."

In sharp contrast to this, is the theory that Alberto braked to avoid hitting something which suddenly ran across the track. Was it one of those black cats, so dreaded by Alberto? Or a hen pheasant, or a rabbit, or a hare, scampering across the Park?

Or could it be that a laborer crossed the track, convinced that there could be no danger as it was the lunch-hour? Certain journalists have even elaborated this theory further suggesting that if the worker had been in the way, then the SIAS (Società Incremento Automobiliasmo Sportivo), for whom he worked and which was responsible for the track, could therefore be officially held to blame. The unproven hypothesis goes on to suggest that, as May 26 was neither a race day nor an official day of practice, the SIAS would not have insured Monza track against the eventuality of one of their workers causing the death of Italy's World Champion race driver. So, rather than pay up the huge sums involved, the SIAS are supposed to have decided to persuade their workman to keep quiet and to let Alberto Ascari's own Life Insurance Company pay up instead.

This incredible story was further elaborated by saying that this workman later confessed to a priest and ended up hanging himself in a mental hospital near Milan, unable to bear the terrible consequences of the death for which he had been responsible.

Mietta has recalled: "Several years later I attended a Spiritualist seance. They invited me, and I went; I did not speak with Alberto, but another spirit came forward who told me, through the Medium, that there was someone who crossed that track, but that Alberto was killed instantly and suffered little pain."

Further theories for the crash related to the driver himself. What if a sudden wind, had made his tie blow up into his eyes, blinding and confusing him at a vital moment? During that week, they had been cutting the grass at Monza. In May and June, Alberto Ascari suffered from hay fever. What if he had had a violent sneezing fit?

Then there was the fact that with the Lancia and the Ferrari, the brake pedal and accelerator pedal are reversed; so had he momentarily forgotten this and pressed down on the wrong pedal? Then the effects of his Monte Carlo ducking, which in Gigi's opinion, "had left him terribly shocked!" Firstly, the stiffness in his right thigh, which meant that at 115m.p.h., you only had to delay one second in your pedal movements and the effect could prove fatal; alternatively a clot could have formed in one of the veins up in his lungs - such an embolism could have rendered him unconscious; then the cerebral embolism - a blood clot from his damaged inner nose - would have also rendered him unconscious.

Next come the psychological effects. Firstly, the absence of his light blue helmet, the talisman mascot of victory, may have made him less sure of himself. For Alberto Ascari was neither the first, nor the last racing driver to be attached to mascots.

In his book, "Speed Was My Life", the German Race Manager, Herr Alfred Neubauer recalled: "I've known very few ace drivers who did not suffer from superstition in one form or another. Hermann Lang's wife always nailed a small horse-shoe to the Pits; on one occasion in the Prix Masaryk at Prague she forgot it and Lang crashed. Tazio Nuvolari wore a golden tortoise with the letter "N" on its back, a present from the famous Italian poet, Gabriele d'Annunzio; Rudi Caracciola's wife was never without their monkey Anatol. . .'

Stirling Moss has explained: "Most of the drivers that I know are pretty superstitious - maybe their reasons are the same as mine - that it costs nothing therefore you might just as well be superstitious as not. I always carried a gold horse-shoe on a chain round my neck, given to me by my sister, and I always tried to wear it the right way up to keep the good luck in it."

Mike Hawthorn's superstitions were a lap ahead. He first wore his blue bow tie with white polka dots, when an ordinary one had flapped in his face. Afterwards he *always* sported a bow tie. He always wore a black helmet and a light green jacket, always pulled his socks up and turned them over twice, always wore his belt which was covered with charms, always climbed into the cockpit of a Jaguar, Vanwall or Ferrari from the righthand side.

Hawthorn, driving for Ferrari, won the World Championship in 1958; that same year, his friend Peter Collins, who would always race with a child's seaside bucket and spade in his cockpit, was killed at the Nürburgring. Hawthorn was deeply upset. He died in January 1959, while speeding along the Guildford by-pass, his 3.4. liter Jaguar going into a violent sideways skid for 100 yards, smashing a bollard in the center of a greasy road, snaking across into the oncoming lanes, clipping the tail of a lorry, ploughing up the grass verge, wrapped itself round a tree and ended up - ironically, in a *hawthorn hedge.*
Archie Brown always wore his yellow-striped, British Racing Green helmet; Graham Hill always carried his rowing colors as an emblem for his racing helmet, while Jackie Stewart always had the Tartan round *his* helmet. An Argentinian racing driver called Carlos Pace started his career by sporting a helmet with an arrow which came from the back over and down to his forehead, and met with no success. Back in the Argentine, Pace is said to have consulted a local guru, who told him to change the direction of the arrow on his helmet so that it was pointing upwards. He did so and his luck changed somewhat. So it goes on. Alberto's attachment to his blue helmet, therefore, was not

so very unique. . .

Finally, we must ask ourselves , whether, as he drove up to Monza that morning, or as he climbed into Castellotti's car at midday, Alberto Ascari was concerned that it was the 26th of the month, and everything that day implied? This was the twelfth and last 26th of the months during which Alberto was 36 years-old. Only another eighteen days and he would by 37 and hence would have lived longer than both St. Antonio of Padua and longer than Antonio Ascari - and those two shadows would have faded away to nothing.

This is neither the first nor the last time that the Mathematics of Coincidence have played a part in influencing a motor-sport event - especially where an accumulation of Thirteens was concerned.

Twenty-five years before, the circumstances surrounding the death of one of England's great racing drivers, Sir H.O.D. Segrave, presented a number of strange coincidences. On Friday June 13, at 1313 hours, Sir Henry and his two mechanics steered the *Miss England II* hydroplane past an islet called Belle Isle and out across Lake Windermere for their speed record attempt. Segrave already knew of another Belle Isle, the lake at his father's old estate near Limerick, Southern Ireland, where as a teenager he had first learned to drive a motor launch.

AUTHOR'S POSTSCRIPT

I am interested in coincidences. In the months before he died, I had been helping my great friend, Leo Villa, formerly Chief Mechanic to Sir Malcolm and Donald Campbell with a book entitled "Life With The Speed King". On his deathbed at Redhill General Hospital, Leo and I arranged that a blue-rimmed steering wheel used by Sir Malcolm and by Donald, and since looked after by Leo, should be presented to the Steering Wheel Club in Curzon Street at the time of book publication.

In December 1979, I therefore arranged for Leo Villa Jr. and Jean Wales (Malcolm's daughter and Donald's sister) to be present at the unveiling of that steering wheel. The only day that Leo, Jean, myself, my publisher and the Secretary of the Club could be present was on January 26.

Among the endless topics that Leo and I had discussed, had been Life after Death. We had once jokingly made a pact that whoever died first would communicate with the other - somehow from the Beyond.

On January 18, precisely one year after Leo's death and some 13 years, 14 days after Donald Campbell's fatal crash in the *Bluebird K7* hydroplane - my literary agent, John Pawsey, telephoned me with an offer to do a biography of Alberto Ascari and his father Antonio. I had just about heard the name. The interested publishing company was Proteus Ltd. The only other context where I had come across the name Proteus, was with Donald Campbell's *CN7 Bluebird,* the Land Speed Record car, engined with a Bristol Siddeley *Proteus* engine.

In my preliminary researches, I discovered some of the coincidences about Antonio and Alberto Ascari, which you may already have read about in the previous pages of this book. Both deaths on the 26th interested me from a family point of view. My grandparents were married on July 26, 1909. My wife and I were also married on July 26, 1978. My wife's maiden name was Alex Albani and she has Italian blood.

On January 24, while doing these preliminary researches, I had my hair cut, locally in a London suburb, by my middle-aged barber, a Greek George Christie, whose shop is across the road from Ferraris. Telling him of my new project, I learnt to my astonishment, that 30 years ago, George, working as an assistant hairdresser at a shop run by Frank Vennosi at 6, Mead Street, Soho, Central London, used to cut and shave an Italian racing driver's hair, and he started to describe Alberto's physical characteristics. The following day I double-checked by showing George a number of uncaptioned photographs of various racing drivers - a sort of identification parade. George picked out Alberto Ascari. So the man who had cut "Ciccio's" hair in Soho in the late 1940's/early 1950's on the few occasions that he was over here, was now cutting the hair of his biographer miles away from Soho...

The Proteus contract arrived on the morning of January 26. The Steering Wheel was duly unveiled that evening. On January 28, I telephoned a Mr. Eason-Gibson, whose father, Secretary of the BRDC and fluent in Italian, had been a good friend of Alberto. Mrs Eason-Gibson answered the phone and when I mentioned Ascari, she immediately said,

"That's strange. He's just been on television."

"Who? Ascari?"

"Yes, a quiz program - they showed an old film of him winning a race."

I reflected on how many times film footage of Alberto Ascari had been broadcast during the past three years.

During February I researched in London Libraries to find out as much as I could in England about this Italian driver. Then on March 15, I went to Milan, Alberto's home city.

That first day at Milano, a Saturday, I was the tourist, trying to get back into the swing of speaking Italian and doing some market research by asking "the man in the street" if he or she remembered the name Alberto Ascari. I strolled into the newly cleaned cathedral and went down some steps into its ancient but recently excavated foundations. Here I met a middle-aged attendant. On an irresistible impulse, I asked him whether he was from Milan. Affirmative. Did he remember the name Alberto Ascari? A strange look came onto his face, and he told me that both he and Alberto had both gone to the same Elementary School together, some fifty years ago, and sat next to one another! So where was this school, I asked? In Via Pietro Moscati. Name of Teacher? Capitano dei Fascisti, De Filippo. Several other questions, all answered, proving that this man was telling the truth... With this meeting, I realized that the coincidences were continuing irrespective of the country in which I found myself.

I had wanted to interview Count Gianni Lurani, the racing driver and historian, a friend of Alberto's, present on the fatal 26th. I had written to him but had not received a reply. I had been told that he would probably be out of the country.

On the afternoon of March 17, I entered the office of Dr. Paolo Montagna at the Milan Automobile Club in Corso Venezia. Dr. Montagna was most helpful, and among the people he suggested I contact was Count Lurani.

"But he's out of the country," I said.

"No he's not, because I saw him yesterday."

Montagna 'phoned Lurani's home. The Count was not at home, but on his way to the Milan Automobile Club to collect his car! Montagna 'phoned to the Car Park below and asked that when Lurani arrived, he should come to the office. Sure enough, Lurani arrives. He has indeed been out of the country for several months - and in several days' time, is due to go away again. He had not even seen my letter as it must be in a pile of still unopened mail. Then and there, I interviewed him. Coincidenza!

I interviewed Mietta and Tonino Ascari on the 18th. Gigi Villoresi, who had been on holiday in Martinique, came back to Milan the afternoon before I returned to England. I was able to record three hours of interview - to me gold-dust.

Fate had reserved one last coincidence for me before I left Milano - possibly the strangest. I was waiting in the Departure Lounge, looking out onto the runways. On my green windcheater, was a yellow pad embroidered onto which was "Spirit of Australia The World's Fastest Boat." Sitting opposite was a man in a black mackintosh and grey trilby hat.

"Are you an Australian?" he asked me. We fell into conversation. He was a businessman. I told him I was writing a book on Alberto Ascari and about my researches. "That's strange," he said. "As you were talking, I felt goose pimples on my arms, because you see, I was up there at Monza, the day Ascari was killed. I can still remember the date. Midday on May 26 1955. I was a 25-year-old student at the time and I had gone up there with my Leica camera to do a photo-study of the park....."

Kevin Desmond
(Cricklewood, London,
England)

APPENDIX I

The Principal Racing Successes Of Gigi Villoresi

1933	Corsa Grossglockner	- 1st. cl.1100 su Fiat
1937	Coppa Mille Miglia	- 1st cl. 1500 su Lancia
	Circuito di Albi	- 1st ass. su Maserati
	Coppa Acerbo	- 1st cl. 1500 Maserati

Nell'anno 1937 e stato campione italiano conduttori classe 1500 categoria corsa

1939	G.P. del Sud Africa	- 1st ass. su Maserati
	Targa Florio	- 1st ass. su Maserati
	Circuito del Carnaro	- 1st ass. su Maserati

Nell'anno 1939 e stato campione italiano conduttori classe 1500 categoria corsa

1940	Targa Florio	- 1st ass. su Maserati
1946	G.P. di Nizza	- 1st ass. su Maserati
	Circuito di Voghera	- 1st ass. su Maserati
1947	G.P. di Buenos Aires	- 1st ass. su Maserati
	G.P. di Nizza	- 1st ass. su Maserati
	G.P. di Strasburgo	- 1st ass. su Maserati
	G.P. di Losanna	- 1st ass. su Maserati
1948	G.P. di Buenos Aires	- 1st ass. su Maserati
	II G.O. di Buenos Aires	- 1st ass. su Maserati
	G.P. di Napoli	- 1st cl. 2000 s. su Osca
	G. P. d'Inghilterra	- 1st assoluto
	G.P. Pena Rhin	- 1st su Maserati
1949	Circuito di Interlagos	- 1st su Maserati
	G.P. di Bruxelles	- 1st su Ferrari
	G.P. di Lussemburgo	- 1st su Ferrari
	G.P. di Roma	- 1st su Ferrari
	G.P. d'Olanda	- 1st su Ferrari
1950	G.P. Evita Peron	- 1st su Ferrari
	Circuito di Rosario	- 1st su Ferrari
	Circuito di Marsiglia	- 1st su Ferrari
	G.P. di Erlen	- 1st su Ferrari
	G.P. Autodromo	- 1st su Ferrari
1951	Circuito di Siracusa	- 1st su Ferrari
	G.P. di Pau	- 1st su Ferrari

	G.P. di Marsiglia	- 1st su Ferrari
	Mille Miglia	- 1st su Ferrari
	Circuito Lido d'Albaro	- 1st su Ferrari
	Circuito di Senigallia	- 1st su Ferrari
	G.P. del Valentino	- 1st su Ferrari
1952	G.P. di Modena	- 1st su Ferrari
1953	Circuito di Sicilia	- 1st su Ferrari
	G.P. dell'Autodromo	- 1st su Ferrari
	12 Ore di Casablanca	- 1st su Ferrari
1954	G.P. di Porto	- 1st su Lancia

APPENDIX II

The Principal Racing Successes of Antonio Ascari
1923   1st. Cremona Circuit
        2nd. Targa Florio
        3rd. Circuit of Mugello
1924   1st. Italian GP.; Cremona Circuit
        2nd. Italian Touring Car G.P.
1925   1st. European G.P.

The Principal Racing Successes of Alberto Ascari
1947   1st. Modena Sports Car Race
        2nd. Cairo Cisitalia Marque Race
1948   1st. Pescara G.P.; San Remo G.P.
        2nd. British G.P. (Maserati)
        3rd. French G.P. (Maserati)
1949   1st. Italian G.P.: Swiss G.P.; International Trophy,
              Silverstone; Coupe des Petites
              Cylindrèes, Rheims; Bari G.P.; Peron G.P. Buenos
              Aires. (Maserati)
        2nd. Lausanne G.P.
        3rd. Belgian G.P.: Autodrome G.P.: Monza: Rosario G.P.
1950   1st. German G.P.; Coupe des Petites Cylindrees,
              Rheims, Mons G.P.; Penya Rhin G.P.; Circuit of
              Garda: Modena G.P.; Rome G.P.; Luxembourg
              G.P.; Peron G.P.; Buenos Aires; Mar del Plata G.P.
        2nd. Italian G.P.; Monaco G.P.; Marseilles G.P.;
              Autodrome G.P.; Monza.
1951   1st. German G.P.; Italian G.P.; Modena G.P.;
              Autodrome G.P.; Monza; Naples G.P.; San
              Remo G.P.; Sestinieve Rally with Villoresi,
              (Lancia Aurelia)
        2nd. Belgian G.P.; French G.P.; Carrera Panamericana.
1952   1st. Belgian G.P.; British G.P.; Dutch G.P.; French
              G.P.; German G.P.; Italian G.P.; Comminges
              G.P.; la Baule G.P.; Marseilles G.P.; Pau G.P.;
              Syracuse G.P.; St. Gaudons G.P.
        3rd. Rheims G.P.; Modena G.P.

1953 1st. Argentine G.P.; Belgian G.P.; British G.P.; Dutch
           G.P.; Swiss G.P.; Bordeaux G.P.; Pau G.P.;
           Nürburgring 1000 Km.
      2nd. Casablanca 12 Hours.
1954 1st. Mille Miglia
1955 1st. Naples G.P.; Valentino G.P.